11/15/19

To: Jim

Game
Of
Life
First
Keep having fun with
this great Game.

Warmest Aloha!

Claude is one of the top instructors in the game today. His willingness and ability to provide his students with comprehensive coaching (short game, course management, mental skills, etc.) is a rare find among golf instructors, many of whom simply provide basic technical swing analysis. Claude's insights are sure to help you take your game to the next level.

Dr. Rick Jensen
Sport Psychologist in Golf
Clients include more than a dozen Major Champions from the PGA and LPGA Tours
Author of *Drive to the Top!* and *Easier Said Than Done*

Golfers of all ages and abilities will benefit from Claude Brousseau's expertise. This book is an outstanding resource filled with excellent information on the short game designed to help you play better golf and have more fun!

Henry Brunton, B.P.E.
PGA of Canada Master Professional
GOLF Magazine Top 100 Teacher
Author of *High Performance Golf* and *Journey to Excellence*

Claude has a masterful understanding of the short game and the ability to communicate easily with golfers of all skill levels. I use him for my own game every time I can!

Mark Sweeney
Inventor of AimPoint® Golf Green Reading System
Coach of three #1 ranked tour players in the world

Claude's book is a must read if you want to improve your short game skills. He masterfully provides basic yet powerful techniques to help golfers of all skill levels. Claude is not only a great teacher but a brilliant communicator. This is not just a "How to" book, but a book that helps golfers use their skills on the golf course. His tactical approach of "Taking it to the course" will definitely take strokes off your game.

Dana Rader
LPGA Master Professional
1990 LPGA National Teacher of the Year

Claude's energy and work ethic is world class. His hunger for learning and expanding his competence in all areas of the game is extraordinary. He constantly takes action and creates quality programs and coaching for any golfer coming his way.

Pia Nilsson and Lynn Marriott
VISION54 Co-Founders
Golf Digest's 50 Greatest Teachers
Ranked #1 and #2 Female Instructors in America

In golf, you want to hit the sweet spot! In life, you want to hit the jackpot! I was fortunate to recruit Claude Brousseau PGA Master with the PGA of America. Claude has great credentials, a super personality and a work ethic second to none. You REALLY want him to coach you. Your game will improve drastically!

Jean-Claude Forestier
Owner of Golf PGA France du Vaudreuil

REALIZE
YOUR
GOLFING
POTENTIAL

Unlock the SECRETS of a PROficient Short Game!

CLAUDE BROUSSEAU
PGA MASTER

Cover design and layout by Apostle's Landing, Bayfield, WI
Text design and layout by Apostle's Landing, Bayfield, WI

Thank you to *Golf Magazine France* for providing the design inspiration.

Traduction from French in collaboration with Georges Guilleminot www.efstranslations.com

Photographs by Philippe Millereau www.kmsp.fr
Photographs by Frédéric Froger www.imagesgolf.com

ISBN: 978-0-9907631-7-8
Library of Congress Card Catalogue No.: 2017943616

First Printing September 2017

Sea Script Company
info@seascriptcompany.com
206.390.6628
Seattle, Washington

SEA SCRIPT COMPANY
BOOK PUBLISHING

CONTENTS

FOREWORD

It is with great pleasure that I write the Foreword to this book.

I have known Claude Brousseau for over twenty years. He first came to see me for help with his own game, seeking information and guidance. It was obvious right there and then that Claude had a great passion for the game and an intense desire to improve.

Since that time, I have seen him grow immensely as a golf instructor and as a person. He now teaches in Hawaii and France and helps players of all levels improve and enjoy this game.

In reading Claude's first book, *Realize Your Golfing Potential*, you can expect to understand short game concepts, practice helpful drills to ingrain new motion and learn to "Take it to the course."

This is a masterful collection of thoughts and images which will let you chip, pitch, hit sand shots and putt with increased confidence, leading to lower scores.

I have enjoyed this work greatly, as I know you will too.

Wishing you great golf,

Martin Hall
Host of *School of Golf* on Golf Channel
2008 National PGA Teacher of the Year

ACKNOWLEDGMENTS

This book is the result of great collaborators.

Of course the influence of my mom, Jeanne D'Arc and my dad, Raymond, was major. You shaped the essence of my personality and character. You planted the seeds of perseverance and the desire to be "The best I can be." You taught me to be altruistic, to respect everybody and to adapt to any situation. For that I will always be truly grateful.

Jean-Claude Forestier owner of "Domaine du Vaudreuil" had the vision of establishing the first short game golf school in France. Thank you so much for giving me the opportunity of a lifetime to create the Golf Court Academy. You and Veronique constantly enrich my life. I treasure your friendship, which is irreplaceable to me.

Christian Lambert, an accomplished journalist, was the initiator of my great relationship with Guy Barbier, former Editor-in-Chief of *Golf Magazine France*. Your support was essential in this adventure. Guy saw the potential of communicating the concepts of golf in many ways and opened the door to this collaboration.

Barbara and Tony Magnall revised and corrected my second language misspelling and grammatical double and triple bogies. Your friendship and all the good memories in North Carolina as well as the Masters and Hawaii are priceless.

Ludovic Pont, Editor-in-Chief of *Golf Magazine France*. You have been instrumental in the success of the "Hors-Série Technique. Spécial Petit Jeu 124 pages pour mieux scorer," the foundation of this book. It is such a privilege to work with you.

Philippe Millereau and Frédéric Froger, your talent and ability to take the best pictures make it fun to work with you. Thank you for catching the best of my numerous swings.

BIG MAHALO! Chris Noda who initiated the opportunity of realizing my dream of teaching at Kapalua Golf Academy.

The thousands of golfers in the U.S., Canada, France, Belgium and Luxembourg who trust my expertise, I can never thank you enough for the privilege of coaching you and sharing my knowledge. You motivate me to keep learning, and you are the reason I enjoy pushing the limits of my competence every day.

To all the teachers, coaches and guest speakers I've had the pleasure to learn from through the decades of summits and conferences I've attended, you have shaped my philosophy of coaching people to play better golf and to have fun with "The Best Game in the World."

To Beth Farrell of Sea Script Company, without your wisdom and support this book would never have seen daylight. Thank you so much for your expertise.

"Fore the Love of the Game!"

INTRODUCTION

Like many of you, golf was not my first sport. I needed something fast and physical so squash was my chosen sport. After several injuries, my doctor suggested golf as an alternative. It was an eye-opener! I was hooked immediately and it soon became my passion. So I did what passionate people do and bought a golf course in 2008.

I have a profound admiration for athletes who perform at the highest level, and I receive immense pleasure from playing in pro-am tournaments where I am privileged to enjoy and experience a lifestyle inside the rope.

I enjoy golf for the challenge the game offers, the sportsmanship, friendship and quality time I get to enjoy with fellow golfers.

I wanted to differentiate and enhance the experience golfers will have at le Golf PGA France du Vaudreuil, the course I own in Normandie, so I developed the idea of creating an academy dedicated 100% to the short game which, I am proud to say, is the first in France. I reached out to the PGA of America to assist me in the process of hiring a Director of Instruction.

In golf, you want to hit the sweet spot! In life, you want to hit the jackpot! I was fortunate to recruit Claude Brousseau, PGA Master with the PGA of America. He is French Canadian and lives in Hawaii. Claude has great credentials, a super personality and a work ethic second to none. Together we have founded the best short game academy (Golf Court Academy) in France.

Since I first met Claude in December 2008 we have spent countless hours on the journey of growing the game and increasing golf knowledge and culture in France. Several thousand satisfied golfers have experienced Golf Court Academy.

Once again golf accomplishes the purpose, creating multiple priceless memories to share for the rest of our lives!

I am certain you will enjoy Claude's first book as much as I have cherished the time we have spent together.

Jean-Claude Forestier
Owner of Domaine Golf du Vaudreuil

This book is dedicated to Anne-Marie Dugré.
You are the love of my life.
You are the "Wind Beneath My Wings."
You always encourage me and you believe in me every day.
You let me be who I am without restriction.
We are definitely the best team in the world.
Thank you so much for just being YOU!

REALIZE **YOUR** GOLFING POTENTIAL

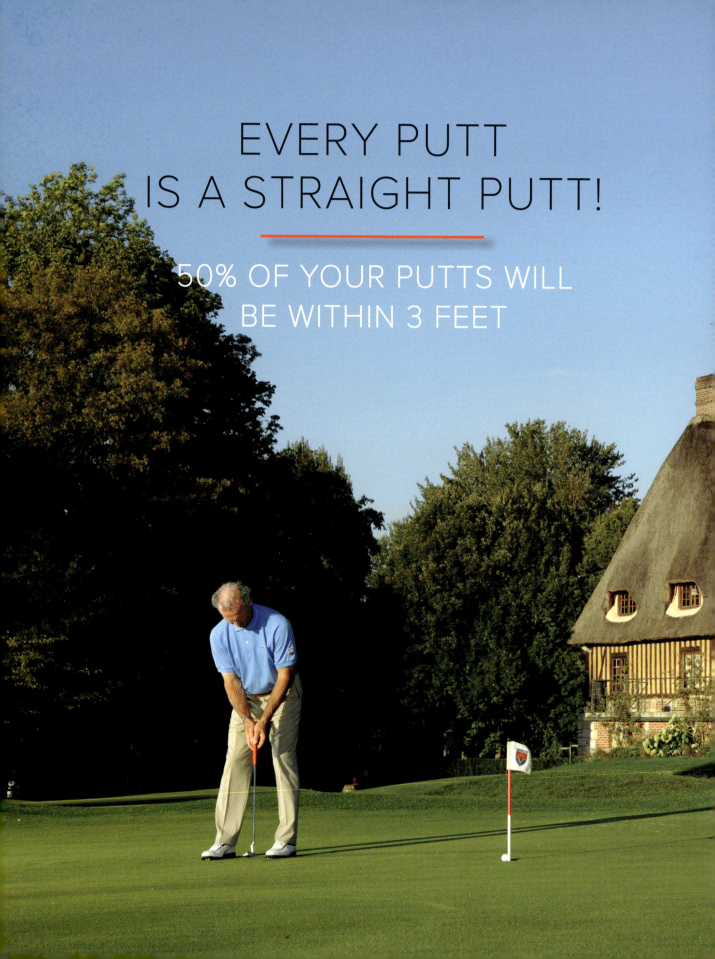

EVERY PUTT
IS A STRAIGHT PUTT!

50% OF YOUR PUTTS WILL
BE WITHIN 3 FEET

Follow these four essential exercises to
MASTER YOUR PUTTING and
LOWER YOUR SCORES

CHECK YOUR BPGA

To be efficient and perform well with short putts, it's important to always set up the same way. To accomplish this, you need to check your BPGA before each stroke: **BALL POSITION, POSTURE, GRIP** and **ALIGNMENT.**

Ball

There are two benchmarks to position your ball:

Horizontally
The ball should be closer to the target foot, about the width of 1 ball off the center of your body (navel).

Vertically
The ball should be under the eye line or slightly inside the eye line, about the width of 1 ball. PROficient golfers do not have their eyes on the other side of the target line.

Line of Play

Posture

The most efficient golfers have a solid, balanced posture when putting.

Weight is distributed evenly on both feet, hands are placed in the middle of the body, arms are hanging relaxed from the shoulders, and shoulders, hips, knees and feet are parallel to the target line. You can have a slightly open stance with the feet, but the arms and shoulders lines should remain parallel to the target line.

Grip

There are various grip styles used by the best golfers in the world. But here is one characteristic that every good putter shares: The grip is diagonal in the palm of at least one hand and the shaft is in line with

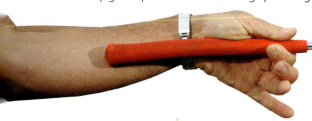

the forearm. In a more conventional grip, both thumbs rest on top of the grip. The amount of pressure is a personal choice. Some players like it very firm, others prefer it more relaxed. The key word here is "constant." Whichever grip you choose, keep it steady. This will help you feel the weight of the putter club head.

Alignment

The putter face must be aimed toward the intended starting line of the putt.

Some of the best players pick a spot a few inches in front of the ball. The intention is to roll the ball over the spot. Keep the head of the putter perpendicular to the ball target line.

You can use a line on the ball to align with your intended line of putt. Use the putter shaft to validate that the line on the ball is correctly placed. On a very short putt, it's best to aim for the center of the hole. If you are not aiming at the center, aim inside of the edges either left or right according to the slope. Don't give the hole away for a margin of security.

A "60 BACK/40 FORWARD" PENDULUM

60% 40%

Get into position. Take a practice swing while looking at the target to determine the amount of energy you will need in your swing to make the ball roll the required distance. The putter face remains square to the path of the swing through the entire stroke. The path of the club will be slightly inside the ball target line on the backstroke and in line with the target line after impact.

The swing-length ratio should be 60% for the backswing and 40% for the follow through. With that swing-length ratio, you will be sure to create a solid impact at the moment of contact with the ball.

Some of the best performers have a ratio of 2 to 1. It takes twice the time to complete the backstroke as it does the forward stroke regardless of the length of the putt. The better golfers take an average of 0.6 seconds to complete the backstroke and 0.3 seconds to complete the forward stroke.

STAY POSITIVE!

On a short putt, you have a 3-ball margin of safety because the diameter of the hole is the width of 3 golf balls. Always believe your ball will roll into the cup. After all, that was your intention!

FIND YOUR PATH

To improve your club path, I recommend using a training aid called the IDL Stroke Putting Track®.

To use the device:

⚑ Find a straight putt and place your ball 5 feet from the cup. Orient the line traced on the ball toward the middle of the hole.

⚑ Place the track parallel to your ball target line so that the heel of the putter touches the inside wall of the device.

⚑ Execute your putt by letting the club head slide along the wall. The shape of the wall will guide your putter head to go slightly inside the target line during your backstroke and stay on the target line during your forward stroke.

⚑ Alternate between a series of putts with and without the track to master the motor skills of an effective swing path.

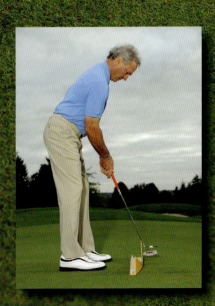

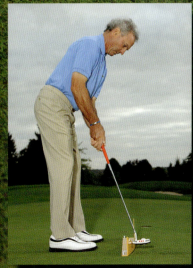

VARY THE SPEEDS

This exercise is simple. Place a tee inside the back of the hole. Using 3 balls, set them up 3, 4 and 5 feet away from the hole. Follow these 3 steps:

STEP 1

Play the first ball with the intention of having the ball roll and touch the tee.

STEP 2

Play the second ball with the intention of having the ball "die" at the front edge of the hole without touching the tee.

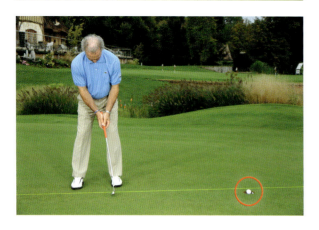

STEP 3

Play the third ball with the intention of having the ball reach the middle of the hole without touching the tee.

Repeat this exercise 2 or 3 times with 3 balls during a training session. It will help you improve your touch and your awareness of the energy required for the distance. It will also provide options from which to choose when facing a flat, breaking, uphill or downhill putt.

PUTTING

THE SWEET SPOT IS THE WINNER!

The ultimate goal?
SINK MORE PUTTS

NUMBER ONE FACTOR:
THE SWEET SPOT!

The most important factor for controlling the speed and distance of your putts is to contact the ball with the middle of the putter face. A poorly centered ball will rarely roll on your intended line of putt, and it will rarely reach your desired distance.

Centering the ball properly means to make contact with the ball on the sweet spot of your putter. Generally, the sweet spot is located in the center of the face and is often identified with a mark.

How do you find the sweet spot?

Your putter may have a dot or a line or two to identify the sweet spot. To find the sweet spot if it's not marked (or to confirm the mark as the sweet spot), take your putter by the handle and make the ball bounce several times on the clubface. Observe the spot where the face remains nice and straight on contact. The bounces will feel solid with no undesirable vibrations. Mark that spot with a felt pen or marker. You've found your putter's sweet spot.

YES
Contacting the ball on the sweet spot will considerably increase the probability for the ball to roll the desired distance. The quality of the contact will be superior and the roll of the ball will be more predictable.

NO
Hitting the ball near the toe of an open putter face makes the distance hard to control, and the ball will roll to the right of the target line.

NO
Hitting the ball near the heel of a closed putter face makes the distance hard to control, and the ball will roll to the left of the target line.

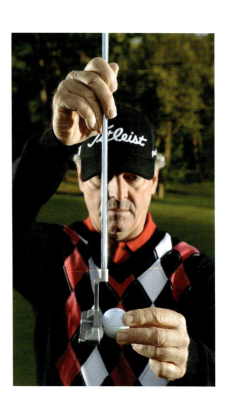

CENTER BETTER WITH THE SWEET SPOT 360®

To practice centering your ball when putting, use the Sweet Spot 360. This training aid sticks and peels off from the clubface easily and provides two types of feedback when the ball doesn't tap on the sweet spot: 1. an auditory feedback, a "muffled" thud on contact, and 2. a visual feedback, the ball rolls sharply to the left or right of the target line.

For this exercise, we suggest you practice on distances of 3 to 5 feet to start, then increase as desired.

Apply the Sweet Spot 360 on your putter face once you've located your club's sweet spot.

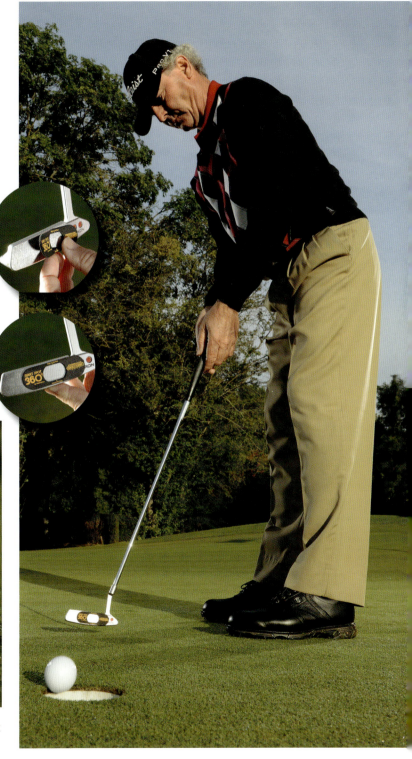

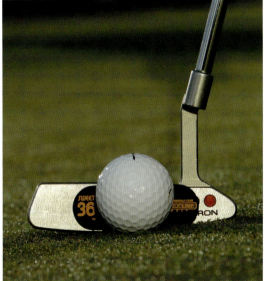

Place the ball at the center of the Sweet Spot 360 and putt.

PUTT WITH
A HEAVY BALL

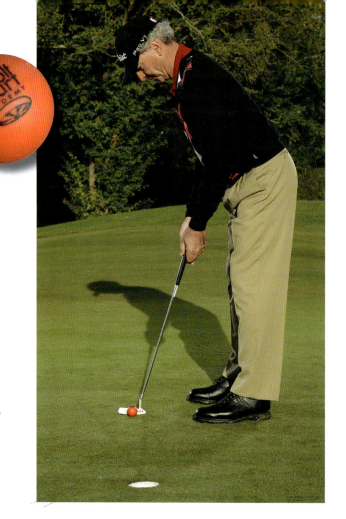

Another great way to learn how to center the ball is to putt with a heavy ball, which weighs five times more than a normal golf ball. This training aid lets you know whether you connected with the sweet spot or not. If you don't center the heavy ball perfectly, it just won't roll! The feedback from this ball lets you know when the energy was transferred optimally by a solid contact on the sweet spot. This is how you will be able to consistently control the distance travelled by your ball.

Putting with a heavy ball is an excellent way to improve how you center the ball.

4. TEST

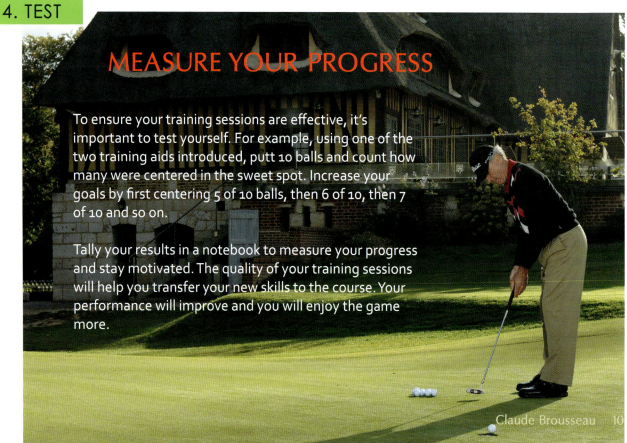

MEASURE YOUR PROGRESS

To ensure your training sessions are effective, it's important to test yourself. For example, using one of the two training aids introduced, putt 10 balls and count how many were centered in the sweet spot. Increase your goals by first centering 5 of 10 balls, then 6 of 10, then 7 of 10 and so on.

Tally your results in a notebook to measure your progress and stay motivated. The quality of your training sessions will help you transfer your new skills to the course. Your performance will improve and you will enjoy the game more.

LET THE PUTTER SWING

LET GO OF CONTROL
TO GAIN CONTROL

When putting, many players over control their swing and attempt to place the putter head perfectly behind the ball at the moment of impact to sink their putt. This method is destined for failure. With the help of several training exercises, you will learn and experience why it's better to let the putter swing naturally.

These concepts were designed to help you improve your motor skills on the greens. You can look forward to seeing the ball rolling into the hole more often!

LESS CONTROL, BETTER PERFORMANCE

Here you will learn that the less you try to control the club at impact, the better you perform! In golf performance, it's important to accept that you need to let go of control to gain control. With this innovative concept, you will learn to avoid controlling the impact. You will keep your movements to a minimum and stick with what's essential. Less is always better in golf.

Technically, the putter's path will naturally come to the inside of the target line, and the toe of the putter will rotate slightly on the backswing. On the forward swing, the putter will track along the same path and the toe will once again rotate slightly in the opposite direction and be square at impact. This all happens with no significant over manipulation by you. After impact, the club can travel in a straight line or slightly to the inside of the target line.

To get a feel for this technique, hold the tip of your putter's grip in front of you using your index finger and your thumb. Without moving your hand, make the putter swing and observe how it sways. You need to feel that same sensation of letting go and avoid over controlling the putter when you putt.

When addressing the ball, the face is perpendicular to the intended target line.

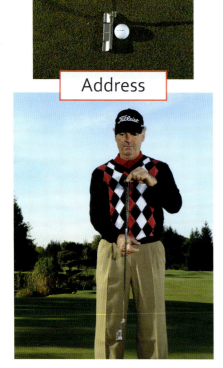
Address

Backswing

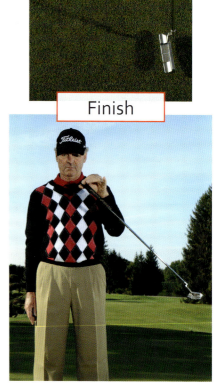
Finish

At the address, the putter face is perpendicular to the target line. We often call this square.

The toe of the putter naturally rotates slightly during the backswing.

Feel the putter swinging forward on its own.

PUTT WITH TWO BALLS!

A good training exercise to learn to let the putter swing freely and release is to putt with 2 balls.
Use 2 balls, a white one and a yellow one.

Place the 2 balls against the clubface as close as possible to the sweet spot. The white ball will be slightly closer to the heel and the yellow ball will be slightly closer to the toe.

Putt by letting the club swing freely. If you do it right, the yellow ball should roll better and farther than the white one. If not, then you're controlling the club too much at the time of impact.

PRACTICE WITH YOUR EYES CLOSED

Putting with your eyes closed is a training exercise that will help you learn how to let the club swing freely. Set up 5 or 6 feet from the hole and putt 10 balls with your eyes closed.

There are several benefits to this exercise:

- It keeps you from adding unwanted motion at the impact.

- It lets you feel what's happening at the impact. Ask yourself, "Did I let the club do the work or did I try to help it along?"

- This is an excellent exercise for correcting the famous yips, those involuntary hand twitches.

LOOK AT THE BALL AND THE HOLE AT THE SAME TIME

We know that it's better to let the putter swing freely rather than try to over control it at impact. To bolster this tactic and increase your putting performance, you will want to focus your mind on your objective, which is the hole. Train by using this approach:

- Once set up at address, look at the hole one last time.

- Take your eyes back to the ball keeping the image of the hole in mind.

- Immediately initiate your swing.

- By doing this, you will remain focused on the target and won't have time to generate unwanted thoughts.

- Develop this approach while training, and then use it on the course.

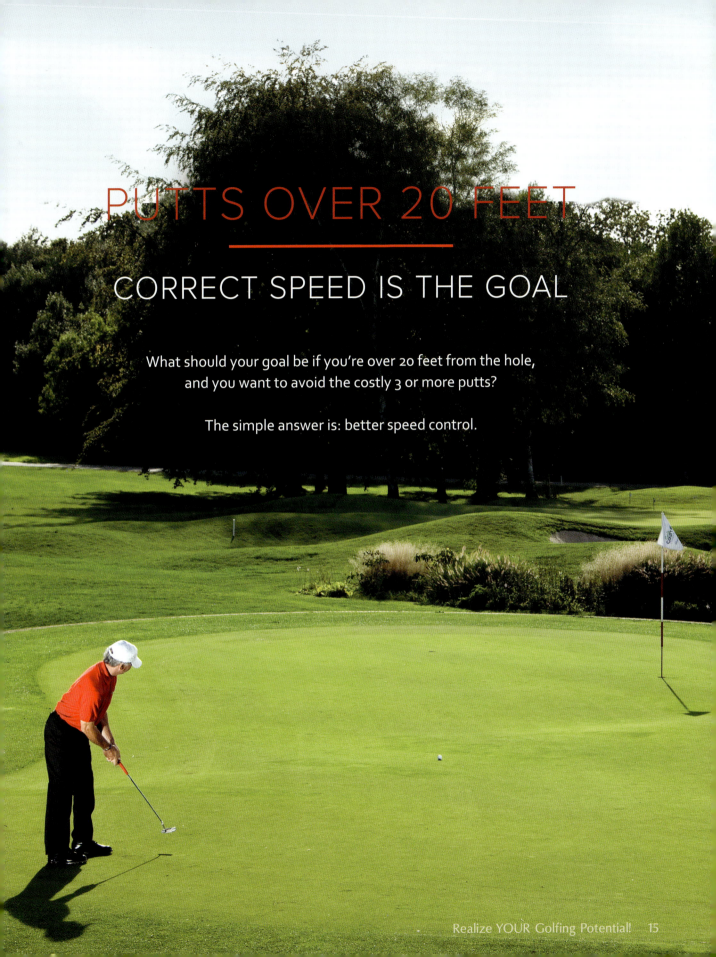

PUTTS OVER 20 FEET

CORRECT SPEED IS THE GOAL

What should your goal be if you're over 20 feet from the hole, and you want to avoid the costly 3 or more putts?

The simple answer is: better speed control.

PUTTS OVER 20 FEET

Every golf shot requires an efficient set up. Make sure your mind and body are ready for action, then focus on managing the tempo and amplitude of the swing. Whether playing a short putt of 3 feet or a long one over 20 feet, it's important to always have the same set up. To do this, you have to check your BPGA: BALL POSITION, POSTURE, GRIP and ALIGNMENT.

With a proper address, perform your swing by keeping the same tempo. On average, with a 3-foot putt, the best players in the world take about 0.6 seconds to complete the backswing and 0.3 seconds to return to the ball. The amplitude, which will create the right speed for impact, will depend on the distance required: The longer the putt, the greater the amplitude. The ratio of backswing/forward swing will remain very similar, meaning 2 to 1.

Posture

Hands are positioned at the center of the body. Shoulders, forearms, hips, knees and feet are parallel to the target line, weight is distributed equally on both feet, eyes are slightly inside the target line.

Grip

The grip is placed more in the palm than in the fingers. The grip and the shaft will be in line with the forearm. In most cases, both thumbs rest on the top of the grip unless you use a claw grip or other variation. There are many ways that lead to success.

Alignment

The club head must be perpendicular to the intended target line.

Ball

Your ball will be positioned approximately the width of 1 ball toward the target foot or leading foot using the sternum or navel as the reference point. Your eye line should be slightly inside the target line.

The swing amplitude will generate the necessary speed for the impact.

Resist the urge of adding useless motions at the time of impact.

Let the energy of the swing carry the putter's head toward the target. The amplitude of the forward swing is almost symmetrical to the backswing.

Here again, avoid the temptation to add something at the moment of contact with the putter head on the ball.

EVALUATE THE DISTANCE

When you're facing a putt of over 20 feet on the course, the first thing to do is to carefully gauge the distance. To achieve this, I recommend taking two steps:

1. Calculate the distance that separates your ball from the hole by walking from the ball to the hole, one large stride representing 3 feet. By doing this, you will have a good idea what the length of the putt is and you will be able to rely on your "distances databank" to feel the amplitude required to roll the ball the proper distance. You can use the number of steps or convert the number of steps into feet.

2. Just before playing, position yourself near your ball and make a few practice swings while looking continuously at the hole. Your visual system will give specific signals to your muscular system to help decide what amplitude and energy are needed for making your putt.

AIM FOR THE TARGET

The main culprit causing 3 putts is poor speed control on the first putt. You have to learn to regulate your speed control for long putts and hit them consistently to within 3 feet of the hole. For this, get a training aid made up of a target and a circle with a 3-foot radius. Place the target hole in the middle of the circle. Set up about 10 feet away on a relatively flat area. Take 6 balls and try to hit them all inside the circle. Once successful, repeat the exercise at 20 feet, and work your way up to 30 feet. Do this training exercise at least once a week to develop your feel and speed control.

ESTABLISH BENCHMARKS

A common question of many amateur players is, "What amplitude should I use for a 20-foot putt?"

It really depends on the type of putt (flat, uphill, downhill) and the speed of the green. To avoid major speed control mistakes, you can expand your personal "distances databank" by making 10 putts at various distances.

Depending on your personality, you have two ways of doing it: You either swing "by feel," using your visual and muscular systems and looking continuously at the hole during your rehearsal shots, or you use a more "technical" approach, by establishing precise benchmarks. For example, you might have to move the putter head just inside your trailing foot to hit a flat 9-footer putt. For a 20-foot putt, it might instead be to just the outside of the trailing foot, then 10 inches outside of the trailing foot for 30-footer.

Finally, remember that the tempo is a crucial element of great distance control, only the amplitude is changing with the length of the putt.

9 feet

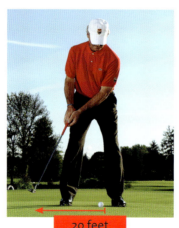

20 feet

30 feet

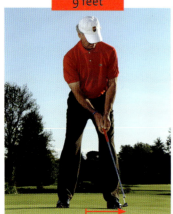

PUTTING

BE MINDFUL OF
YOUR SPEED CALIBRATION

In putting, you often hear the term "Never up, Never in."
If the ball doesn't roll past the hole, it can never go in. To increase your odds
of making a putt, we recommend using a speed which optimizes the hole diameter.

BE MASTER OF THE DIAMETER

There's an ideal speed for all putts, regardless of the distance. If the ball doesn't roll in the hole, it should stop about 15 inches past it. In that scenario, you'll leave yourself with a "gimme" second putt, but more importantly, you'll have given yourself the best odds of making the first putt.

According to the research done by Mark Sweeney on a green of 8 on the Stimpmeter®, if the ball rolls 2 feet past the hole, the cup shrinks to a diameter of 1.9 inches. If it is 3 feet, the cup is down to 1.4 inches. If it is 4 feet, the cup is only 0.9 inches. The probability of make it decreases as the distance past the hole increases. Of course the hole is always 4.25 inches, even if some days it appears either bigger when you are confident or smaller when you are under pressure.

Whatever the length of your putt, attempt to roll the ball past the hole in a zone you feel comfortable in while keeping in mind the above numbers.

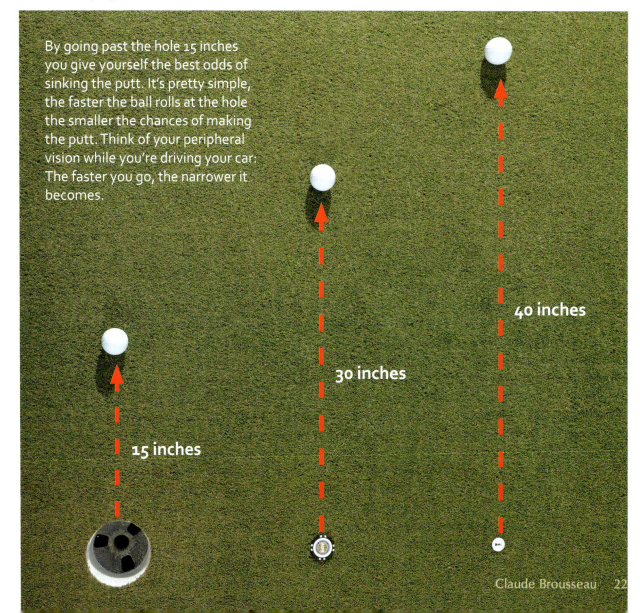

By going past the hole 15 inches you give yourself the best odds of sinking the putt. It's pretty simple, the faster the ball rolls at the hole the smaller the chances of making the putt. Think of your peripheral vision while you're driving your car: The faster you go, the narrower it becomes.

40 inches

30 inches

15 inches

Claude Brousseau   22

IMPROVE YOUR TEMPO

To become PROficient at making long putts or rolling the ball near the hole to have an easy coming back "tap in," you have to learn how to putt with a smooth, continuous swing. Think of a metronome with its steady "tick tick." Never attempt to speed up or slow down your swing at the moment of impact. To the contrary, no matter what the length of the putt is, you have to keep the same ratio of time. The magic ratio to remember: It takes half the time to return at the ball than it takes to complete the backswing. The amplitude of the swing has to change. The longer the putt, the longer the amplitude. The erroneous tendency is adding speed at the last moment just before impact.

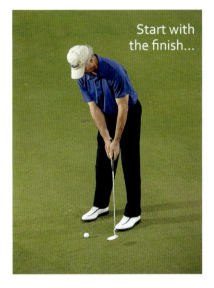
Start with the finish...

...make your backswing...

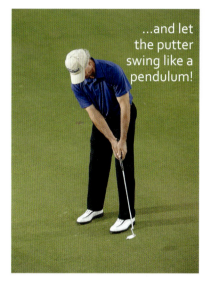
...and let the putter swing like a pendulum!

A good training exercise to improve your putting rhythm is to start your swing where you finish. This very simple exercise will promote a smooth and fluid swing. Repeat it several times to get a good feel for it, and then re-create the same sensation when you putt on the course.

YES
NO

The second exercise I recommend is practicing with the training aid called the Whippy Putter®. This putting aid's shaft necessitates a smooth and fluid swing. If not, the shaft bends and the putter head moves very fast adding too much speed to the ball. If your stroke is fluid, the Whippy Putter keeps its original shape.

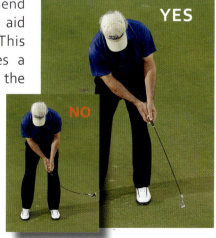
YES
NO

CAN YOU FEEL IT?

In golf, the speed of the greens changes depending on the quality of the grass, the weather conditions and the budget for the maintenance of the course. In short, it's hardly ever the same from one day to the next. To help you tune in your sense for the proper speed control before playing the course, I recommend performing a self-calibration test:

- On the practice green, locate a fairly flat 15-foot putt.

- Do a practice swing while continuously looking at the hole. Your visual system will guide your muscular system to feel what amplitude of swing is required to roll the ball in the hole.

- Make your putt. Before looking up to see where the ball stopped, ask yourself whether the ball went short, long or the appropriate distance. Then look where your ball is. Verify that what you felt corresponds to what actually happened. Keep doing this until your "feel" matches what's real.

Claude Brousseau   24

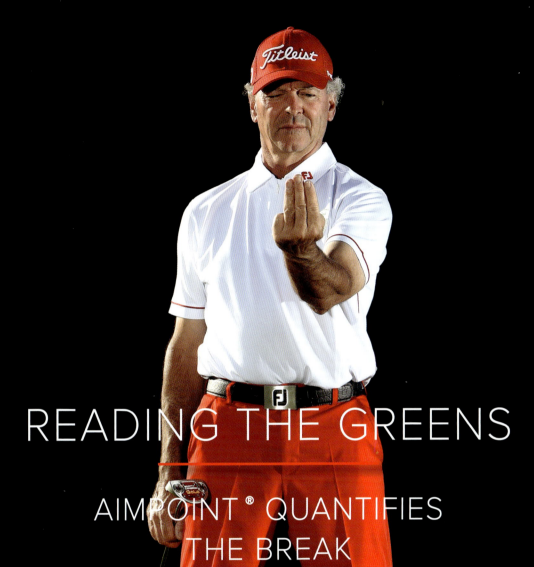

READING THE GREENS

AIMPOINT® QUANTIFIES THE BREAK

Created by Mark Sweeney, AimPoint is a feel base system that has been use by three Number One players in the world. Over 5000 juniors learn with it and more than 150 college coaches use it. It has produced more than 50 wins on major golf tours around the world. Over 45,000 amateurs in more than 40 countries are using it on a daily basis.

THE SIDE TILT OF THE SLOPE

Evaluating the direction of the side tilt of the slope is a very important part of the game. There are so many misconceptions about it including:

- ⚑ The ball breaks toward the sunset.
- ⚑ The ball breaks toward the ocean.
- ⚑ The ball breaks away from the mountain.
- ⚑ The most important part of the putt is the last few inches.
- ⚑ You need to aim at the apex of the putting line.

Do you really think the ball knows where the ocean and the sunset are?

Ask yourself what the single most important factor is that influences how a ball will break on a green. Answer: Gravity. The ball knows the law of gravity. "She" will roll in the direction of the side tilt of the slope regardless of where the sunset, the ocean or the mountains are. This is the most important factor to evaluate first.

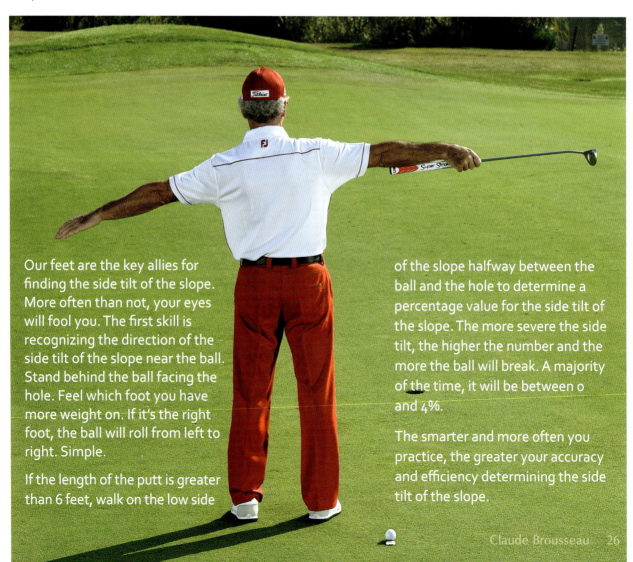

Our feet are the key allies for finding the side tilt of the slope. More often than not, your eyes will fool you. The first skill is recognizing the direction of the side tilt of the slope near the ball. Stand behind the ball facing the hole. Feel which foot you have more weight on. If it's the right foot, the ball will roll from left to right. Simple.

If the length of the putt is greater than 6 feet, walk on the low side of the slope halfway between the ball and the hole to determine a percentage value for the side tilt of the slope. The more severe the side tilt, the higher the number and the more the ball will break. A majority of the time, it will be between o and 4%.

The smarter and more often you practice, the greater your accuracy and efficiency determining the side tilt of the slope.

CHOOSING THE AIMING POINT

Now that you know the direction of the side tilt of the slope, you need to determine a value for the intensity of the slope. You need this information to select the aimpoint. It's time to use your eyes and your fingers. The number of fingers used is the same as the value you have attributed to the severity of the slope. If it's 3, you will use 3 fingers. If it's 2, you will use 2 fingers and so on. The higher the number, the further away from the hole the aimpoint will be.

Place your fingers in front of your eyes to identify the aimpoint.

Place the edge of the first finger in the center of the hole, then look at the edge of your other fingers and you have your aiming point.

READY TO PUTT

Do a few rehearsal swings to feel the energy and the length of the swing required for the distance.

Now you're ready to play!

Aim the putter head perpendicular to a point a few inches in front of the ball on your indented line of putt. If you are using a line on the ball, you will match the direction of the line on the putter with the line on the ball. This line extends to a virtual hole located on the high side of the real hole.

Align your body parallel to this imaginary line keeping your shoulders, arms, hips and feet parallel to the target line. Have a slightly open stand. There aren't many good performers putting with a close stand.

The law of gravity applies as soon as the ball starts to roll. The ball gravitates toward the hole because of the side tilt of the slope.

IMPROVE FAST? PRACTICE SMART!

I recommend using a target hole and a string with two pegs. Place the target hole on your aiming point. Use the string to make a straight line from behind the ball to the target hole. The ball is under the string. You're ready to putt!

Golfers often make the critical mistake of looking at the real hole instead of the virtual/target hole. The most common consequence is pulling the putt and missing in on the low side of the hole. Commit 100% on the target hole.

You may feel the aimpoint is too far from the hole. That's because players typically underestimate the real side tilt of the slope. Make sure your last look is at the virtual/target hole.

Follow these steps and you will see the ball rolling in the hole more frequently, the number of putts per round will decrease, your score will improve and you will have more fun!

CHIPPING FROM THE FRINGE

STICK IT CLOSE!

Here is the best process to make up and down when you've missed the green.
There is no bad side effect to being too good with the fundamentals.

FOUR STEPS FOR A GREAT SET UP

Each golf shot requires a decision and a preparation of your mind and body. I am proposing a 4-step procedure to achieve a PROficient set up every time.

1. Stand with your feet together. Place the ball at the center of your feet. Shoulders, hips and feet are parallel to the target line. The club's grip is pointing to your navel and your arms and hands are hanging relaxed at the center of your body.

2. Move your trailing foot away from the target by the width of one shoe. Keep the rest of your body and the club in the same position.

3. Move your leading foot by 2 widths of your shoe toward the target while remaining parallel to the target line.

4. Move your leading foot back a few inches so that the alignment of your feet is open by 30° relative to the target line, and then rotate that leading foot to the outside. Now put 60% of your weight on that foot. Your sternum and hands will automatically end up slightly ahead of the ball. Your arms will remain in the middle of your body.

Check the following four items:

- The ball is located slightly on the side of the trailing foot in relation to your sternum.
- Your weight is 60% on the leading foot. Your shoulders are parallel to the target line.
- The butt end of the grip is pointing to the navel.
- The face of the club is oriented perpendicular to the desirable line of play toward the imagined landing spot.

PASSIVE HANDS AND WRISTS

Once you're in a good position, you only need to swing your arms while keeping your hands and wrists passive through the stroke. The club must absolutely contact the ball on a downward angle of attack. At impact, the grip has to be ahead of the club head. The shaft has returned to its initial leaned forward angle. The loft of the club will lift the ball for you, which will subsequently roll to the flag. The club's path is slightly inside the target line on the backswing, square on impact and again slightly inside the target line on the forward swing.

A chip from the fringe is made with passive hands and wrists through the entire stroke.

EDUCATE YOUR LEAD WRIST

Many amateurs try to lift the ball at the moment of impact by using their wrists and bending their leading arm. The result is usually a topped or bladed shot. They want to go underneath the ball.

You need a different sensation to minimize the hands and wrists action. I suggest you experience a few shots by wrapping your leading wrist with your trailing hand. This technique keeps you from "adding" any extra motions at the moment of impact.

Perform 5 shots with this unusual set up. Make sure you imprint the quiet feeling of your hands and wrists. Your contact with the ball is more solid. By the same token, your trajectory and distance control improve drastically. Then perform 5 shots with the more conventional set up and your focus is recreating the same sensation.

Claude Brousseau

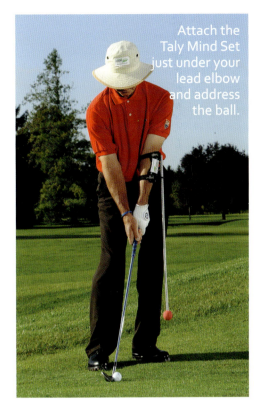

Attach the Taly Mind Set just under your lead elbow and address the ball.

DON'T CROSS THE TALY!

Using the same idea as the previous exercise, here's another way to memorize an effective swing of the arms, wrists and hands while performing a chip shot from the fairway.

Invented by the American, Taly Williams, the Taly Mind Set® is strapped to the leading forearm. The purpose of this training aid is simple: prevent exaggerated wrists and hands motions. This device provides feedback on the PROficient swings as well as the undesirable swings. You learn by experiencing the difference between which swings produce the intended shots.

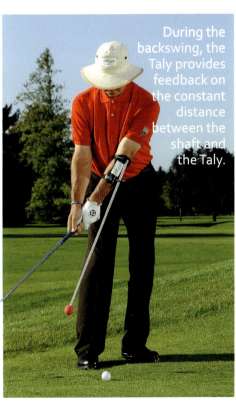

During the backswing, the Taly provides feedback on the constant distance between the shaft and the Taly.

YES

NO

At the finish, the handle of the club will be parallel to the Taly's rod.

CHIPPING EFFICIENTLY

THE SWING PATH
OF SUCCESS

There are many paths to success while you're chipping. Like most golf swings,
if the club travels along an inside-square-inside path you will make great strides.
Simplicity is the mother of comprehension.
It's all about less variables and more predictability.

FOLLOW THE PROFICIENT PATH

When chipping, many amateurs believe they have to swing the club in a "straight line." This means making the club head follow along the intended target line on the backswing and on the follow through after the impact. This technique is not particularly natural and demands unnecessary motions. It can often produce poor contact with the ball. You have all experienced blading it over the green or topping it, and it rolls only a few feet. Even worse, you hit the "big ball" (the earth) before the "little ball" (the golf ball) and chunk it badly.

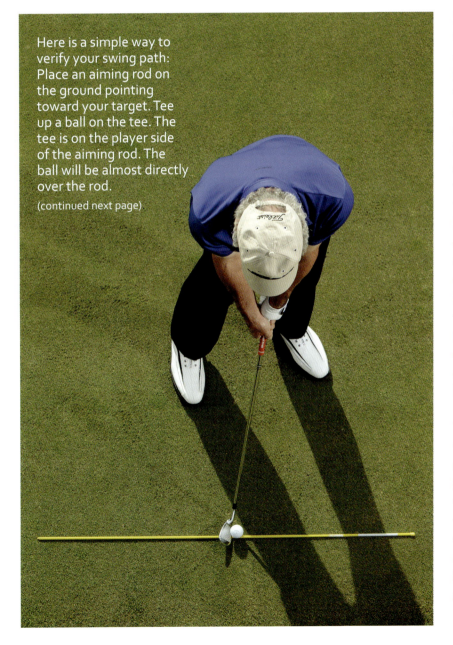

Here is a simple way to verify your swing path: Place an aiming rod on the ground pointing toward your target. Tee up a ball on the tee. The tee is on the player side of the aiming rod. The ball will be almost directly over the rod.

(continued next page)

But if you let the club and your body move as naturally as possible during the backswing, the club head will follow the target line for only a few inches and will ultimately come inside the intended target line. The same goes for the follow through where the club tracks the intended target line just a few inches before and after impact, then turns slightly inward. In fact, the club head travels on a straight line for a very short period of time. Following this path will minimize the risks of a poor contact and increase the odds of getting the ball near the hole.

This very efficient path allows you to maximize the benefit of the bounce. One of the best designers of wedges in the world, Bob Vokey, always tells me, "Claude, bounce is your best friend!" You have to understand that the bounce is your best "insurance policy" against bad contact.

YES

Take a natural backswing. You will find that the club comes progressively inside the target line. We learn by experiencing the difference between several sensations. If you attempt to produce a backswing by forcing the club head to move over the aiming rod, you will feel it's a much more complicated and difficult movement.

NO

Make the forward swing feeling the weight of the club dropping on the ball. Let the club swing inside the target line. Again you should feel this swing path produces a more efficient and effortless motion. It's unnatural to push or direct the club straight over the aiming rod. If you do, you will generate wasted motions and introduce unnecessary variables.

YES

NO

THE HOOP PROVIDES THE SENSATION!

There are multiple ways of training your mind and body to produce an efficient swing. The more senses you have involved in the learning process, the faster you will attain your goals.

At address, the hoop is tilted parallel to the club shaft.

To get a good feel and to memorize how your club should travel, get a plastic hoop (available from major sports stores) and set up as if you were going to play a short chip shot. Hold your club with the trailing hand and the hoop with the lead hand. Tilt the hoop to make it perfectly match the shaft angle. The golf swing is on a tilted plane.

Once in position, make your chipping swing. Let the club slide/glide on the hoop from beginning to end. Repeat this exercise several times to imprint the feeling of the path your club travels on. You can even do this exercise with your eyes closed, it increases the sensation. You're building a pathway in your brain.

THE NAVEL IS YOUR ALLY

Another exercise to feel how your body and club must work together when chipping is to practice a few swings with the grip pressed against your navel. By regularly repeating this exercise, you will feel how the club travels along an inside-square-inside path. Doing this, you will realize it is impossible for the club to travel on a straight line on the backswing as well as on the forward swing. Golf is a "side on" sport. You will feel a very efficient swing path. The arms, the wrists and the hands are quite passive. Again, less is more in golf. Minimize the variables.

Press the handle against the navel.

The rotation of the body leads the club to the inside of the target line.

On the return, it's the same thing. The body's rotation brings the club back to the inside of the target line.

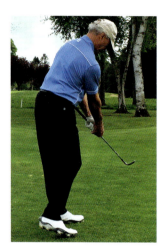

TARGET CIRCLE

To progress more quickly, I recommend splitting your training sessions in two: The first part is to improve your technique (using the exercises introduced earlier) and the second part is to measure your progress. For example, place a 3-foot diameter circle around the hole and set up about 30 feet away. Use 10 balls. Chip each ball and feel how your club follows an inside-square-inside path. Then count how many balls finished inside the circle. Start over by changing the distance and the club, recording your results each time and checking your progress over a period of two weeks or two months depending on how much time you have for practicing and playing. Have fun in the process of getting better. It is a journey not a destination. Enjoy the ride!

Play 10 balls and count how many end up inside the target circle. You will be great at up and down on the course, you will have more fun and your scores will improve.

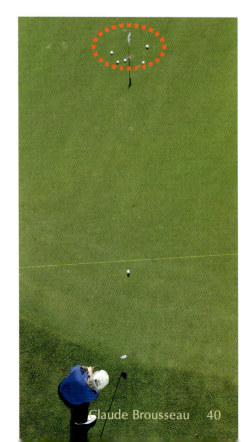

CHIPPING FROM THE ROUGH

PREPARATION IS CRUCIAL

Chipping from the rough is a challenging situation. However, with the proper technique, you will increase the probability to make up and down.

SPECIAL ADDRESS IN THE ROUGH

I suggest placing the ball closer to the trailing foot. The clubface should be oriented toward the intended target. The rough will have the tendency to grab the hosel resulting in the clubface oriented to the left of the target at impact. You could choose to make an adjustment, and set the clubface slightly to the right of your target line at address.

A chip from the rough requires a special address. Here, even if the rough is thick, the idea is to contact the ball first as much as possible. As with any short game shot, you have to check your BPGA: BALL POSITION, POSTURE, GRIP and ALIGNMENT.

- **BALL POSITION** To strike the ball first, the ball must be set closer to the trailing foot. The thicker the grass, the further back the ball must be. In certain situations, it could even be placed outside the trailing foot.

- **POSTURE** The butt end of the club should be pointed to the center of the body, the weight of the body shifted about 60% to the lead foot. The spine angle should be straight up and down. Avoid leaning or tilting away from the target.

- **GRIP** You have to use the same grip as with a full swing. The grip pressure must be steady. In this situation, I recommend you tighten your hands a bit more because the rough can change the direction of the clubface at the impact.

- **ALIGNMENT:** The face of the club must be oriented toward the target yet slightly open for two reasons: To let the bounce facilitate the club head slide on the grass, and to compensate for the closure of the face typically caused by thick grass. The shoulders are parallel to the target line, but the feet and hips are aligned to the left of the target line.

WELL PREPARED AND READY TO SWING!

On this shot, you have to create speed with your arms. Once you're well positioned at address, feel your arms come down "in free fall" with no pulling or pushing. By doing this, you will generate the necessary club speed to yield a solid impact. Your hands and wrists do. . .nothing! Avoid the temptation to scoop the ball up by either overusing the wrists and hands or by shifting your weight on the trailing foot. You have to trust the loft. The bounce will make the club slide in the rough.

On the backswing, the motion of the hips is limited, the weight of the body stays on the leading foot and the wrists remain passive.

At the finish, the navel is oriented to the left of the target, and the club grip is still at the center of the body.

On the downswing, let the club head fall onto the ball. Avoid any effort whatsoever.

STOP SCOOPING THE BALL!

You're playing golf not scooping ice cream! When they need to chip from the rough, many amateurs try to lift or scoop the ball. Nothing can be more counterproductive! By doing this, they destroy the swing radius which is the distance between the sternum and the club head. It must remain constant through the entire swing. A good way to correct this flaw is to train with the ChipInABLE®. This training aid lets you feel when your arms remain fully extended during and after the impact.

At address, place the ChipInABLE between the lead shoulder and the lead hand.

With the ChipInABLE, there's no extra motion during the backswing.

If you attempt to scoop the ball, the distance between your arms will change and the ChipInABLE will get shorter. The club head is closer to the sternum and you will top the ball.
(see round inset)

PLANT THE TEE!

With all the shots played around the green, amateurs are often solely fixated on the ball. The following exercise has a dual objective—"forgetting" the ball and achieving a downward angle of attack, which is a prerequisite for making good contact with the ball in the rough. The principle is very simple: Plant a tee 3 inches in front of the ball and make a chip shot with the intention to either send the tee flying or push it deeper into the ground. If the exercise is done well, your ball will lift perfectly in the air!

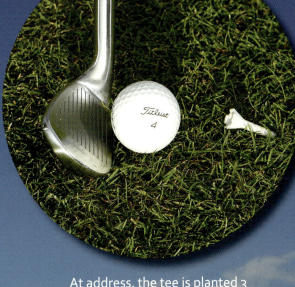

At address, the tee is planted 3 inches in front of the ball.

Position yourself at address in an area of very short grass, and plant a tee 3 inches in front of the ball.

During the backswing, the wrists and hands remain passive.

The club head sends the tee flying and the ball takes off perfectly. Your focus is on the process of swinging the club efficiently instead of lifting the ball. The loft of the club is doing all the work for you. Your ball will end up close to the hole and you will need only 1 putt. One more par saved! This is good for your score and even better, it's fun!

CHIPPING FROM A DOWNHILL SLOPE

NO MORE DESCENT INTO HELL!

Correctly play a downhill approach near the green,
a delicate shot that demands an exact and adapted technique.

IN THE DIRECTION OF THE SLOPE

Around the green you don't always have the possibility to play approaches with your feet level. It's common to find yourself on a slope uphill, downhill, ball above the feet or ball below the feet. The approach on a steep downhill is one of the most dreaded shots for amateurs. The secret of this shot resides primarily in how to set up efficiently. You must adapt to the type of slope you are dealing with. Basically, you want to adjust your body to be in the same direction as the slope.

It is essential that your shoulders and hips are parallel with the slope. We often see amateurs place their hips with the slope, but the shoulders aren't at the same angle. This often results in topping and blading the ball.

We recommend playing the ball slightly closer to the trailing foot.

You don't have too many options with the body weight. It's primarily shifted to the leading foot.

SWING AT THE SAME ANGLE AS THE SLOPE

Avoid the temptation to lift the ball. Once in position, just rock your arms slightly back and forth. Wrist action must be reduced to a bare minimum. A common mistake is to try to lift the body and the hands. The ball will follow a low trajectory because the slope reduces the club's loft angle. The ball contact is the same as for a normal stroke: first the ball, then the ground. You need to adjust your club selection. Most of the time you will select a club with more loft. The ball will fly lower than if you were on an even lie and will roll for a longer distance when it hits the green. You will select a landing zone closer to you.

CHECK YOUR POSTURE

When you're practicing, a simple way to check if your posture is PROficient is to use an alignment stick. Once you're in position at address, put the stick at your hips and then at your shoulders to verify that they're BOTH parallel to the slope.

It's very uncomfortable to have the shoulders tilted in the same direction as the slope. This is why golfers forget to adjust the shoulders. The hips and the shoulders MUST be aligned with the angle of the slope.

SWING UNDER THE ROPE

To feel the type of swing you need for a downhill approach, you can set up an elastic cord attached to two metal skewers above your target line. This time, the goal of the exercise is to swing without the club touching the cord. You will succeed if you keep your wrists relatively passive and by keeping your spine at a steady angle.

By keeping your body steady with passive wrists, the club doesn't touch the cord either on the backswing or the follow through.

NO

NO

If you modify your spine angle either on the backswing or even worse, if you're trying to lift the ball on the follow through, the club will touch the cord in both directions. You will have immediate feedback that this motion is not efficient.

CHIPPING WITH THE BALL BELOW & ABOVE THE FEET

TO SUCCEED, BE FLEXIBLE AND ADJUST

Golf is a game in which you have to adapt. Every shot is a new adventure. You have to learn how to adjust with the different slopes around the green.

BALL ABOVE YOUR FEET

Aim right, stand taller, shortened club and more rounded swing! For any shots played on a slope, the basic rule to be effective is to adapt your address and your swing to the landscape. If the ball is above your feet, it is closer to you. The ball always flies in the same direction as the slope. If you're confused, picture dropping a ball on the slope on which you're playing. What direction will the ball roll? It will do the same in the air. Or picture water running on the slope. In which direction is the water running? The ball will do the same in the air.

There are a few basic adjustments: Aim will be slightly to the right, your body a bit more upright and your hands lower on the grip. Once in position, execute your swing while paying attention to two things: Keep the wrists relatively passive, and perform a more "rounded" swing, which will "hug" the slope more. Finally, be aware that the ball will travel in the direction of the slope, in this case, to the left. It is more pronounced if you have more loft on the club.

To maintain balance, the body is a bit more upright than for a standard swing.

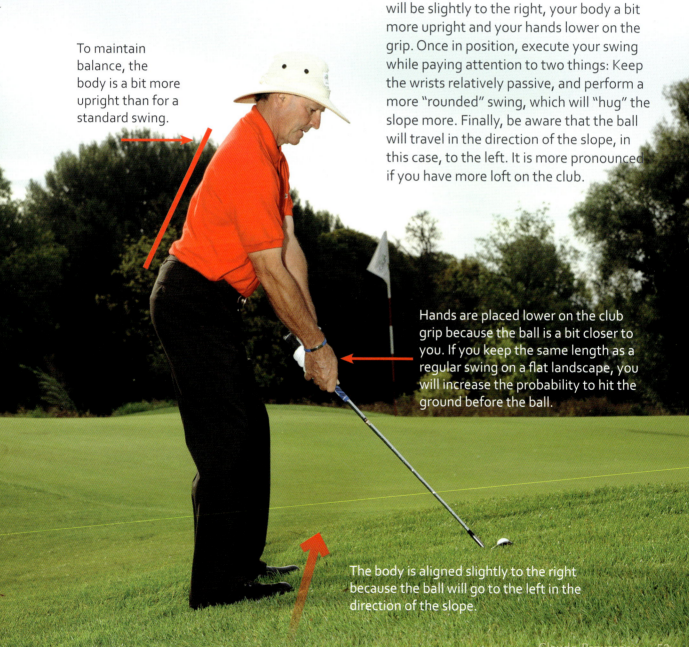

Hands are placed lower on the club grip because the ball is a bit closer to you. If you keep the same length as a regular swing on a flat landscape, you will increase the probability to hit the ground before the ball.

The body is aligned slightly to the right because the ball will go to the left in the direction of the slope.

FLATTER SWING PLANE

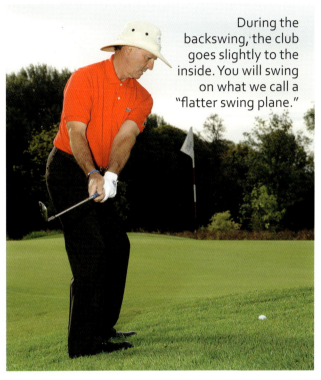

During the backswing, the club goes slightly to the inside. You will swing on what we call a "flatter swing plane."

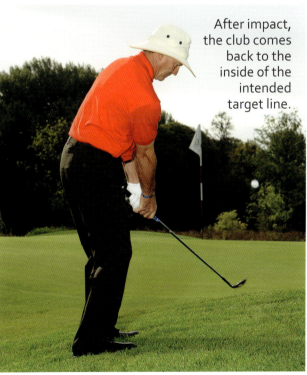

After impact, the club comes back to the inside of the intended target line.

Avoid the temptation to lift the ball.
The loft of the club will do the work for you. Trust the loft!

Slide your hands lower on the shaft. You always want to practice a swing in a situation similar to what you will face when you strike the ball.

Perform some back and forth swings keeping the club against your body. Then re-create the sensation by performing a few approaches on the slope. Be sure to remember all the good shots you made!

BALL BELOW YOUR FEET

Make sure you feel you're keeping your spine angle through the shot. The most common mistake is to raise your torso, which typically results in a topped ball.

Aim left, squat down, lengthen the club, a more upright swing! In a situation where you make an approach with the ball below your feet, the secret to success once again resides in the preparation, which is adapted to the situation. This time, there are basic adjustments: alignment slightly to the left, more flex in the knees, hands at the top of the grip. You should feel very grounded and in balance. Here the challenge is staying down through the shot.

Next, you need an upright swing path. The ball is lower and further from you.

Your hands should be placed at the top of the grip because the ball is a bit farther away. You want to make sure you have enough length in the club to make a solid contact on the ball.

You will feel your knees bent more in a squatting position in order to maintain good balance.

Your body should be aligned more to the left because the ball will "travel" in the direction of the slope, which is to the right.

LET THE CLUB SLIDE TO DETERMINE IF IT'S VERTICAL

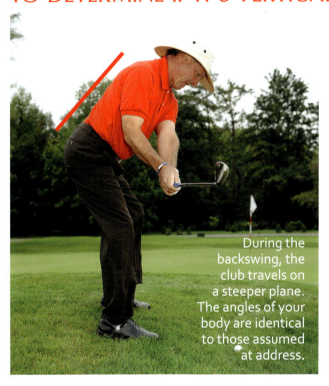

During the backswing, the club travels on a steeper plane. The angles of your body are identical to those assumed at address.

After impact, the angles of your body haven't changed. You have remained "low" throughout the swing.

Here is a simple exercise to help you feel how an upright swing should feel.

Set up on a slope where the ball is below your feet.

Perform your backswing and at the midpoint of your backswing, let the club slide straight down in your hands. If your backswing is sufficiently vertical, the tip of the grip has to be pointing just ahead of the tip of your feet. Repeat this exercise several times to imprint the feeling. Now you're ready to perform your shot. Watch the ball stop very close to the hole. Once again, you have saved your par. Way to go!

CHIPPING

HOW A BETTER CONTACT
PRODUCES A BETTER RESULT

It's all about the quality of the
contact on the ball. To improve
the quality of your chip, you have
to learn how to strike the little ball
(golf ball) first and the bigger ball
(planet earth) second.

HANDS ARE NATURALLY FORWARD

When chipping, you've often been told that your hands must be ahead of the ball. That's true, but they shouldn't be *too* far ahead. In fact, with the design of the club, they're already in front of the ball.

If you place your hands too far forward, you're introducing unnecessary variables. You're creating too much forward shaft lean. This action reduces the bounce. You increase the probability of digging the leading edge of your club into the ground. The bounce is your BEST friend around the green.

You're also reducing the loft of the club. It makes it more difficult for the ball to get airborne, and you risk changing the orientation of the clubface either to the left or the right of your target. All these actions increase the chances of chunking, topping and shanking it. In other words, everything you want to avoid.

To assume the more efficient stance at address, you have to place the club's original loft and bounce angles as naturally as possible. These are your two best friends, they are your greatest assets and your best insurance policy against bad shots. Automatically your hands will end up slightly ahead of the ball. As for your weight, it's shifted 60% to the leading/target leg. From this set-up/original position, it will be a lot easier to contact the ball correctly.

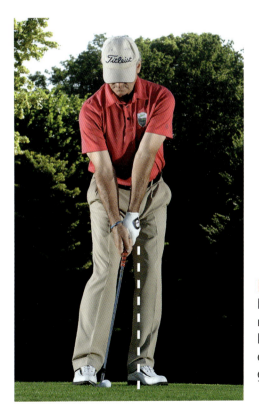

YES The club is well positioned in respect to its loft and bounce. The hands are naturally ahead of the ball. The weight is distributed 60% on the leading leg.

NO Here the player has his hands too much ahead of the ball. It makes it more difficult to achieve good contact.

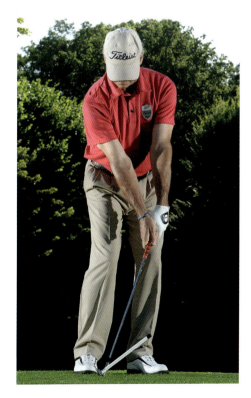

SWING AROUND YOUR LEFT HIP

Once you have a good stance, everything gets a lot easier. You want to produce a symmetrical length motion each side of the ball. In other words, the backswing height equal to the height of your follow through swing. Hands and wrists are passive during the entire swing. Your weight stays mostly on your lead leg throughout. Let the club's loft naturally lift the ball.

During the backswing, rotate your upper body while keeping 60% of your weight on the lead leg.

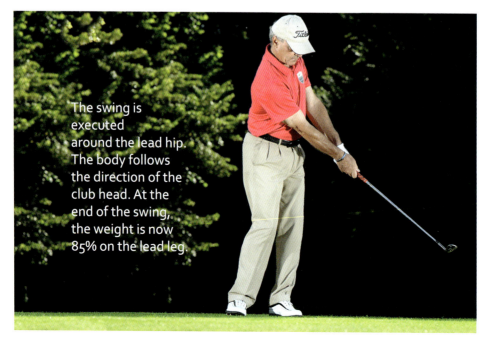

The swing is executed around the lead hip. The body follows the direction of the club head. At the end of the swing, the weight is now 85% on the lead leg.

PRACTICE ON ONE FOOT

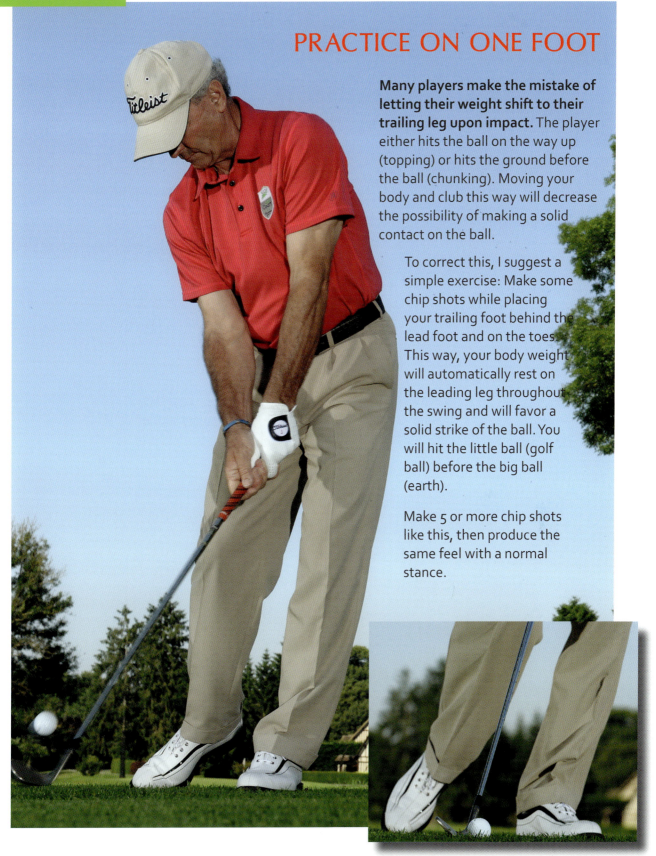

Many players make the mistake of letting their weight shift to their trailing leg upon impact. The player either hits the ball on the way up (topping) or hits the ground before the ball (chunking). Moving your body and club this way will decrease the possibility of making a solid contact on the ball.

To correct this, I suggest a simple exercise: Make some chip shots while placing your trailing foot behind the lead foot and on the toes. This way, your body weight will automatically rest on the leading leg throughout the swing and will favor a solid strike of the ball. You will hit the little ball (golf ball) before the big ball (earth).

Make 5 or more chip shots like this, then produce the same feel with a normal stance.

MEMORIZE THE FINISH

Players sometimes lose their confidence under the pressure of competition. After a few missed shots, they start to over control the club in an attempt to place it perfectly on the ball. This strategy is often counterproductive and paralyzes the athlete. This is an exercise to change the focus of attention as well as the feeling in your body.

Start with the end in mind. Take the address position and, without a backswing, go to the finish. Hold the position for few seconds. You can even close your eyes to increase the sensation. Initiate the backswing from there and return to the finish. Repeat the process 2 or 3 times. Then execute a chip shot with your attention solely on reproducing the feeling of the finishing position. The quality of club/ball contact will increase drastically.

From your address, go directly to the finish and hold there for 5 seconds.

Claude Brousseau   60

4 CLUBS, 4 TRAJECTORIES

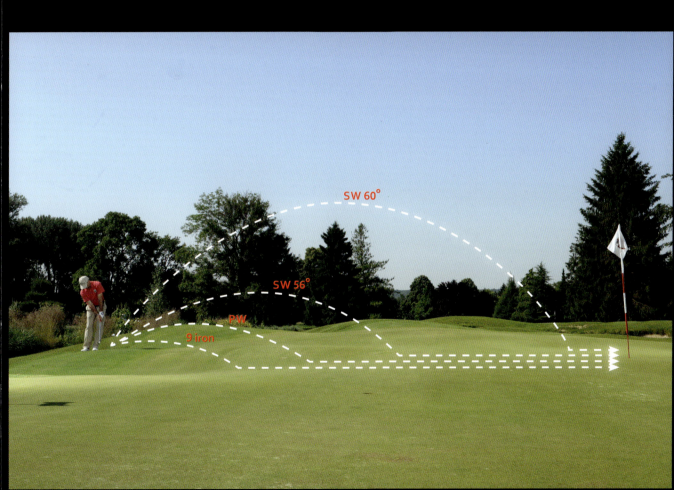

SW 60°

SW 56°

PW

9 iron

PITCHING

SYNCHRONIZE YOUR UPPER AND LOWER BODY

In this lesson, you will learn how to master pitching shots between 30 to 60 yards. You will also learn how to synchronize your upper and lower body during the swing.

MASTER THE PIVOT PERFECTLY

Our wedges are used for shots of 30 to 60 yards for precision, not power. Most amateurs lack consistency because they utilize too much of their arms and hands. In reality, to be precise with length, direction and trajectory, it is more efficient to utilize the big muscles of your body. In others words, you must synchronize the actions of the upper and lower body to produce the desired shot on demand.

On the backswing, your arms and hips are moving together at the same speed.

Keep your upper body and the arms relaxed.

Hands should be positioned just inside of your lead thigh.

The position of the ball should lie in the middle of your body or slightly off-center toward the trailing foot

Make sure your lead foot is slightly open. It will help for an easier follow through.

The swing has the same amplitude on the back and forward swings. You finish the swing with a complete hips rotation. The club and your arms are well centered with your navel.

HOW TO SYNCHRONIZE YOUR PITCH!

Practice as many half swings as possible with a club resting in the palms of your hands. By doing this, it will give you the feeling of a truly synchronized and compact upper and lower body. These two parts work in harmony. The results: major improvement in your ball striking.

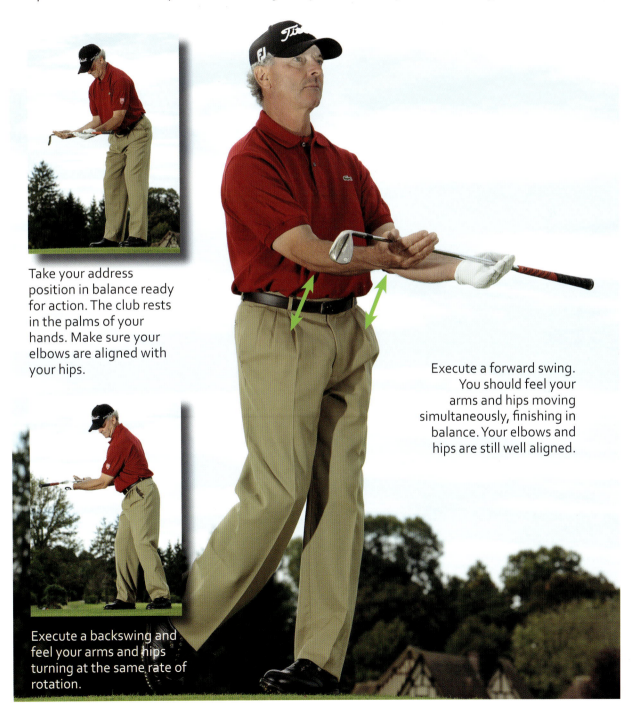

Take your address position in balance ready for action. The club rests in the palms of your hands. Make sure your elbows are aligned with your hips.

Execute a forward swing. You should feel your arms and hips moving simultaneously, finishing in balance. Your elbows and hips are still well aligned.

Execute a backswing and feel your arms and hips turning at the same rate of rotation.

USE THE WEIGHT OF THE CLUB

Pitching shots require very little force. To be precise, you must utilize the pivot of your body and the weight of the club. Here is a 4-step exercise to understand and feel an efficient swing.

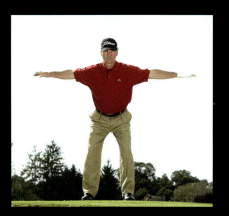

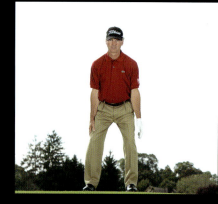

1. **Feel the weight of the arms.** Stand in your golf posture. You are in balance and ready for action! Lift your arms parallel to the ground. Let them fall. Feel the weight of your arms and the speed they generate. This should take no effort whatsoever.

2. **Feel the weight of the club.** Take the same posture as Step 1, but this time you have a wedge in your trailing hand. Let the club fall without trying to control it. Maintain a constant grip pressure. Feel the weight of the club as it is falling. You'll notice that the club is always hitting the ground at the same spot, unless you attempt to over control it. Let gravity do the work for you. Avoid pushing or pulling on the club.

3. **Feel the rotation.** Place a tee centered between your feet. Let your arms fall and simultaneously rotate your body. The club will automatically clip the tee without any extra manipulations. Notice the pivot and the club dropping are doing all the work for you. Feel the weight of the arms, feel the weight of the club, feel the rotation and feel an effortless swing through the ball.

4. **Feel the efficiency of an effortless swing with the ball.** Place a ball on the tee. Let the club "find the ball" with an effortless swing. Watch the ball flying toward the target. Feel the very small amount of work that is needed to strike a golf ball.

FIND THE IDEAL MUSCLE TENSION

It's crucial that you develop tension awareness during your pitching shots. Remember, you need precision not power. I recommend this exercise to find what level of tension produces the best results.

Complete 10 pitching shots between 30 to 60 yards and change your tension level between each swing.

Play the first ball with a lot of tension (picture left), the second ball being very relax, a third ball with a tension in between the first and the second (picture right).

Remember the ball is less than 2 ounces and should travel a short distance in the pitch shots.

Repeat these motion sequences with the 3 balls multiple times keeping track of your results. Which level of tension produces the best performance? Use this level on the golf course!

Swinging with a lot of tension vs. swinging with less tension.

PITCHING

IT'S A SHORT SHOT, KEEP YOUR ARM SHORT!

It's a fact of life. You have more fun if you play better golf! Golfers need to have a reality check. Here are some interesting statistics from the book *Every Shot Counts* by Mark Broadie.

If your average score is:

- 85, you will on average hit 5 greens in regulation.
- 90, you will on average hit 4 greens in regulation.
- 95, you will on average hit 3 greens in regulation.
- 100, you will on average hit 2 greens in regulation.

So if you want to save your par or at least make only bogie, you should improve your pitching motion. This is a very important shot to master. It provides the opportunity to make only 1 putt, or worst-case scenario, 2 putts.

When you miss the green, you will often find yourself 30 to 60 yards from the flag. The worst nightmare is "chunk it" or "blade it" over the green. One of many important aspects of the pitching motion is keeping the trailing arm short. The tendency is extending it too early, and then you pay the price.

A "SHORT" TRAILING ARM BEFORE IMPACT

When playing 30 to 60 yards from the flag, the ball will spend more time in the air than rolling on the green. With this type of shot, one of your technical objectives must be to keep a "short" trailing arm before impact. Executed with efficiency, you have a high probability of generating an effective club path and a more consistent "club/ball" contact. In other words, you will improve your precision, but also improve control over distance and trajectory.

For a normal trajectory shot, at address the ball is played in the middle of your body or very slightly toward the trailing foot. Your posture is athletic and balanced. You can choose a weight distribution of 60% on the lead foot and 40% on the trailing foot.

The backswing is shorter than a normal full swing. You still need a synchronized pivot. Your hands are about hip height to establish a distance referential.

Just before impact, your trailing arm is still slightly bent and in front of your trailing hip.

At address, the ball is in the middle of your feet. Your posture is athletic and balanced.

The backswing is short with a synchronized pivot. Your hands are at the same height as your hips.

Just before impact, your trailing arm is slightly bent and in front of your trailing hip.

Claude Brousseau

AVOID AN "OVER THE TOP" SWINGING PATH

The most common swing flaw in this shot is an early extension of the trailing arm. The cause is often that the golfer is anxious to hit the ball and wants to go underneath to lift it up.

The other cause is that often the golfer initiates the downswing with the upper body first. This almost guarantees a poor contact. It will definitely require an athletic adjustment and it brings less predictability to the shot.

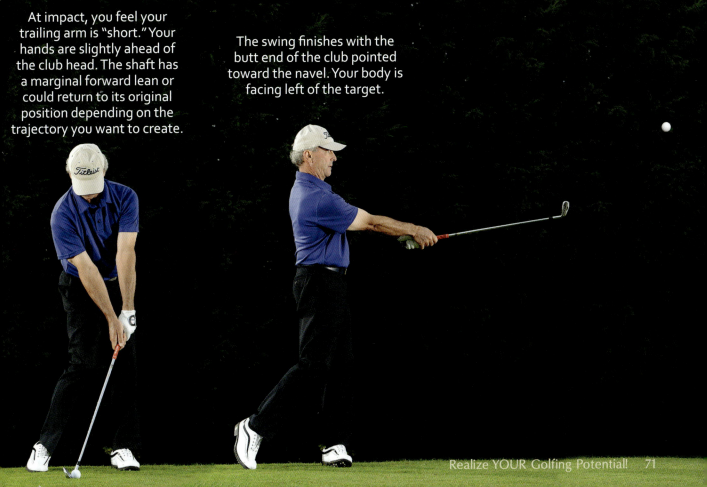

At impact, you feel your trailing arm is "short." Your hands are slightly ahead of the club head. The shaft has a marginal forward lean or could return to its original position depending on the trajectory you want to create.

The swing finishes with the butt end of the club pointed toward the navel. Your body is facing left of the target.

GOLF AND A BOXING GLOVE

What does a boxing training glove have to do with golf? To exaggerate the feel of how your trailing arm should work with your pivot on a pitching shot, imagine yourself wearing a flat boxing glove on the trailing hand. If you want the punching bag to fall over, you have to achieve maximum power at the moment of impact. If you extend the trailing arm too early in the sequence, you will miss the punching bag. If you initiate the movement with the shoulders only, you will also miss the punching bag.

This training exercise will teach you how an effective golf swing feels while performed with minimal effort. The human brain is very smart. I've tested several hundreds of golfers with this exercise. They automatically do a very efficient motion. The sequence of the lower and upper body is always good. They all arrive "square" with the glove at the moment of impact. NOBODY attempts to "scoop" like they do with the club and the ball. NOBODY has an extended trailing arm at the impact.

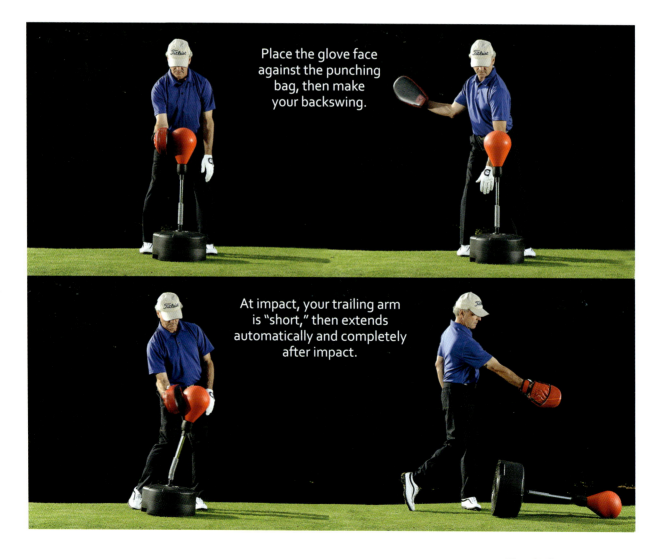

Place the glove face against the punching bag, then make your backswing.

At impact, your trailing arm is "short," then extends automatically and completely after impact.

SIMULATE THE IMPACT

To get a feel of the position of your clubface when it strikes the ball—while practicing or on the course—do this exercise as often as possible. Stand at address without a club. Clench your lead fist (this represents the ball) and press your trailing palm (acting as the clubface) against your lead fist. Make a short backswing turning your shoulders and hips together.

Next, while keeping your trailing arm "short," do a forward swing. As a result, your trailing hand will hit your lead fist solidly every time.

That point represents the moment where the club strikes the ball. You will realize and feel that you have zero wasted motion and that it's very easy to repeat this swing. Now you're ready to transfer this motor skill to your golf game.

At address, the trailing palm is against the lead fist.

Make a short backswing.

At impact, the trailing palm will be perfectly flat against the lead fist.

A DIVOT AFTER THE TEE

As we've previously seen, to generate a precise and consistent trajectory, your trailing arm must be "short" just before the impact. A good training exercise to verify this is to set up a tee and take a swing with only your trailing hand. The goal is to make the tee fly and make a divot past the tee. In fact, the bottom of your swing has to be a few inches on the target side of the tee.

If you make a divot before the tee, you will "chunk" the shot. This will be proof that your arm was extended too early in the swing sequence.

Once you master this training exercise with the tee, use a ball to experience a solid contact.

The club initially hits the tee, then the ground. The divot is made beyond the tee.

THE PITCH & RUN

A 2-STEP APPROACH

It's important to master the Pitch & Run, a shot that's half chip and half pitch that involves pitching the ball onto the green and letting it roll to the flag. A shot commonly used by professionals on every tour in the world, the Pitch & Run is a big time shot saver on any course you will play.

BALL IN THE MIDDLE, POSTURE DYNAMIC

The Pitch & Run is the perfect shot when you have a lot of green to work with. This is often the best option because it provides greater room for error without being too penalized. Around the green the ground is your friend. You want the ball to roll as much as possible. Golf balls are round for a reason, they're meant to roll.

You perform a Pitch & Run when there isn't a big obstacle to go over and the hole is located toward the end of the green. The idea is simple: Select a landing zone toward the beginning of the green. Fly the ball to the zone and let it roll to the flag from there.

To execute this shot correctly, first prepare the best you can by checking your BPGA: **BALL POSITION, POSTURE, GRIP** and **ALIGNMENT.**

BALL Use the sternum or navel as a reference point for the ball position instead of the width of the feet. Most of the time with the Pitch & Run, the ball will be placed slightly toward the trailing foot. Be careful not to overdo it. It makes a huge difference in golf to move the ball the width of 1 ball!

POSTURE This is just as dynamic as for a full swing. The keyword with posture is always BALANCE. The weight should be equally distributed on both feet. Some players prefer having marginally more weight on the lead foot.

GRIP Use a normal full-swing grip. Remember, the ball is less than 2 ounces. The amount of muscular tension in the grip allows you to feel the weight of the club head. The keyword is a STEADY, relaxed grip pressure.

ALIGNMENT The clubface is aligned toward the intended starting line of flight. Shoulders are parallel to the target line. The leading foot is set back a little from the trailing foot. If you flair out the leading foot, it will make it easier to finish the swing fluidly.

MINIMIZE HAND MOTION

Once in a good position, it's time to think about executing the swing. Rehearse a practice swing while staying focused on the feel/sensation of the motion. The objective is to keep hand and wrist motion to a minimum and emphasize the body's rotation.

During the backswing the rotation of the body pulls the hands, which could go as high as hip level if the green is very long, then you just unwind your body toward the left of the target. You will feel the weight of the club dropping on the ball. The momentum will carry you through to the finish. The club points left of the target. You will feel a complete body rotation. Most of your weight will end up on the leading foot. You must finish in balance.

This shot can be played with a pitching wedge, a 9 iron or an 8 iron. A lower loft angle will result in a lower trajectory and more roll. The club selection is dictated by the total distance and the trajectory you want.

At the top of the back-swing, how high the hands go depends on the club selection and how far the hole is from the beginning of the green.

Finish by turning your body left of the target.

At the finish, most of your weight is on the lead leg. The triangle initially formed between the arms and club has been maintained. You will be able to go back to the address position and need very little adjustment to strike the next ball. If you have to greatly manipulate the club to re-create the address position, you know you had some wasted movement in your swing and were losing accuracy.

KEEP THE CLUBS PARALLEL

Many amateurs tend to use their arms or hands too much when they hit a Pitch & Run causing a number of errors related to contact, distance and direction.

To correct this tendency there's a good training exercise, which consists of swinging 2 clubs and keeping them about 2 feet apart from each other. The challenge is to keep the distance constant from the address to the finish.

This exercise, practiced without a ball, will help you improve the rhythm of your swing. You will feel the synchronization of your upper and lower body.

Remember this is a "Precision with Finesse Shot." You don't need a ton of power.

Set up at address, a club in each hand. The distance between the 2 grips and the 2 club heads should be about 2 feet. The tendency will be not having enough distance between the clubs.

Perform your backswing until your hands are level with your hips. The distance between the 2 clubs hasn't changed. If you're overusing the trailing arm, the distance will increase.

Swing forward to the finish position keeping the distance constant between the clubs. If you're overusing the trailing arm, you will bang the forward club.

PUSH THE WOODEN BLOCK

Here's a training exercise to help you understand the role of the body's pivot motion when hitting a Pitch & Run. The most common mistake is the golfer stops the pivot. They'll overuse arms, hands and wrists only.

Set up at address, the clubface against a wooden block.

Create the impact position with shoulders square, hips open and your weight on the lead leg.

Get a brick-size wooden block and place it against your clubface when setting up at address. Simulate the impact position—hips slightly open, weight on the lead leg, the shaft leaning slightly toward the target. Go ahead and complete the rotation. The wooden block moves forward. Without doing too much with your hands and wrists, continue your pivot motion to achieve the finish position.

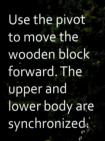

Use the pivot to move the wooden block forward. The upper and lower body are synchronized.

Repeat this exercise several times. Make sure you mentally embed the feel of it. You will use the same pivot motion when you're out on the course.

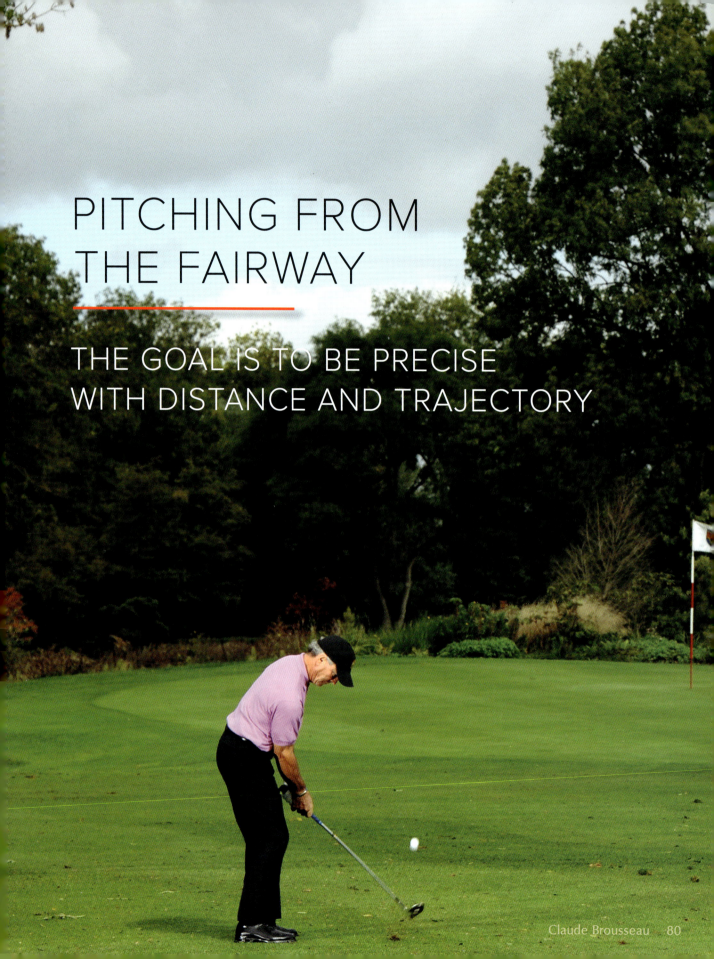

PITCHING FROM
THE FAIRWAY

THE GOAL IS TO BE PRECISE
WITH DISTANCE AND TRAJECTORY

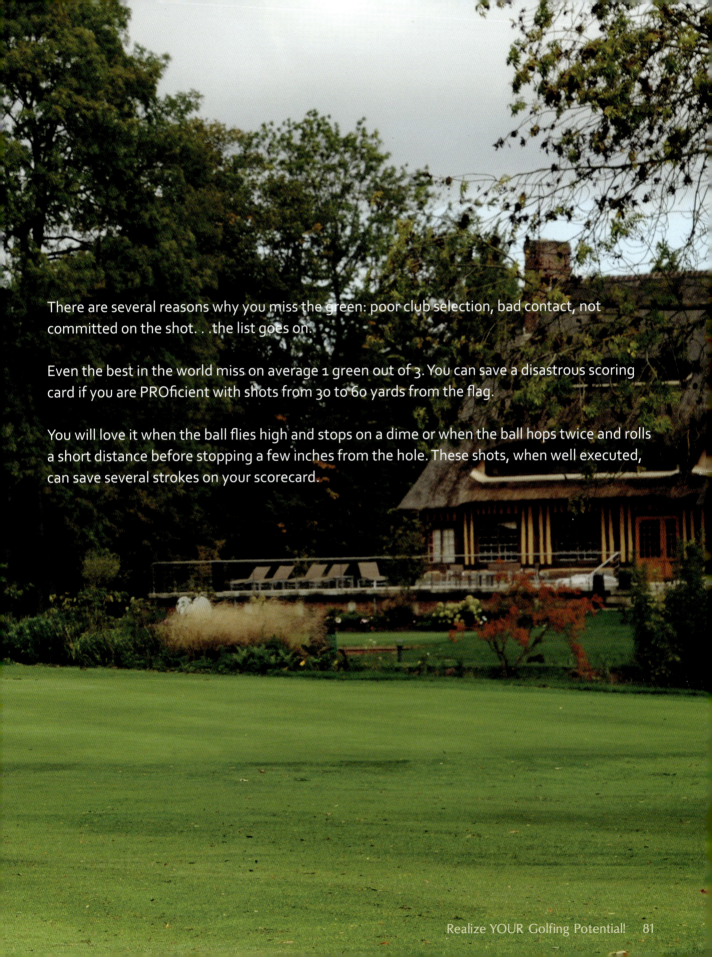

There are several reasons why you miss the green: poor club selection, bad contact, not committed on the shot. . .the list goes on.

Even the best in the world miss on average 1 green out of 3. You can save a disastrous scoring card if you are PROficient with shots from 30 to 60 yards from the flag.

You will love it when the ball flies high and stops on a dime or when the ball hops twice and rolls a short distance before stopping a few inches from the hole. These shots, when well executed, can save several strokes on your scorecard.

BALL SLIGHTLY BACK, BODY SQUARE

While taking your stance when pitching (as for all short game shots), it's important to check your **BALL POSITION, POSTURE, GRIP** and **ALIGNMENT.**

If you can set up for each shot while focusing on those four points, you will improve your effectiveness and consistency.

Alignment The club head is facing the target. Your body (feet, hips and shoulders) is parallel to the target line. You may prefer to be slightly open with your feet and hips.

Grip Use your normal full-swing grip. The pressure must allow you to feel the weight of the club head and must remain constant.

Posture Weight is distributed evenly to both feet or you may prefer slightly more weight on the lead foot. Feet are spread about the width of your hips. You need to be in balance.

Ball position Ball is slightly toward the trailing foot.

A SYNCHRONIZED AND FULL ROTATION

Once in position, your goal is to swing, feeling your hips and shoulders rotating together on the backswing as well as on the follow through. In essence, the pitch shot requires a body pivot and not just your arms. Keep in mind that the shot can be played with a wedge for which the loft can vary between 46° and 60° depending on the trajectory and distance you want.

Hips and shoulders make a synchronized rotation.

On the backswing, feel your hips and shoulders turn away from the target. Avoid using the arms only. At the end of the follow through, your belt buckle faces left of the target and the sole of your right shoe is completely exposed.

A DIVOT AFTER THE LINE

If you regularly top or chunk the ball when pitching, here's a great exercise to improve your ball strike. You simply trace a white line using baby powder on the grass at your practice area. You set your ball on the line with the goal of making a divot on the target side of the line.

Thanks to your descending angle of attack, the club head strikes the ball first then the grass. The bottom of the swing will be a few inches in front of the ball. This way you can control the distance and the trajectory of your ball.

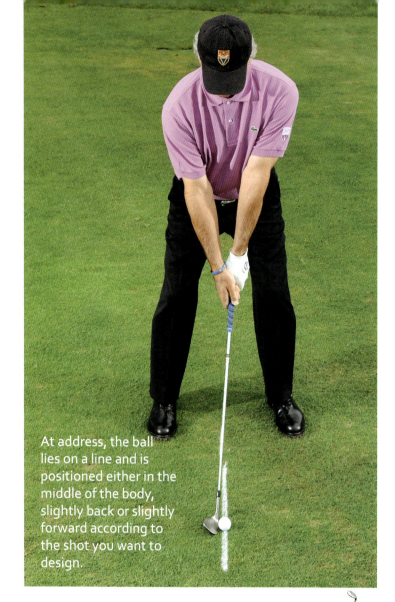

At address, the ball lies on a line and is positioned either in the middle of the body, slightly back or slightly forward according to the shot you want to design.

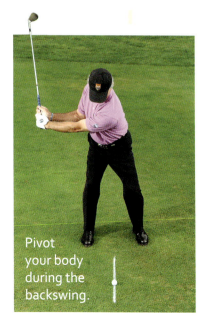

Pivot your body during the backswing.

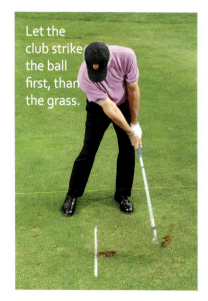

Let the club strike the ball first, than the grass.

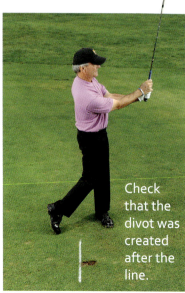

Check that the divot was created after the line.

AVOID THE NOODLE!

The following training exercise helps you memorize a more efficient club path by avoiding an over the top path. For this, you will use a common training aid: a swimming noodle attached to an alignment stick. You will place it behind and above your ball in perfect alignment with the target line.

Parallel to the target line, place an alignment stick (here in yellow) or a club which lets you visualize the "square" alignment of the feet, hips and shoulders.

Once set up, the goal of the exercise is to make a pitch shot without touching the noodle, both on the backswing and the follow through. With a bit of practice, you will learn the suitable club path.

The club must avoid touching the noodle on the backswing and the downswing. If you come over the top, from the outside to the inside, the club will touch the noodle!

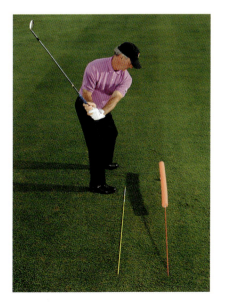

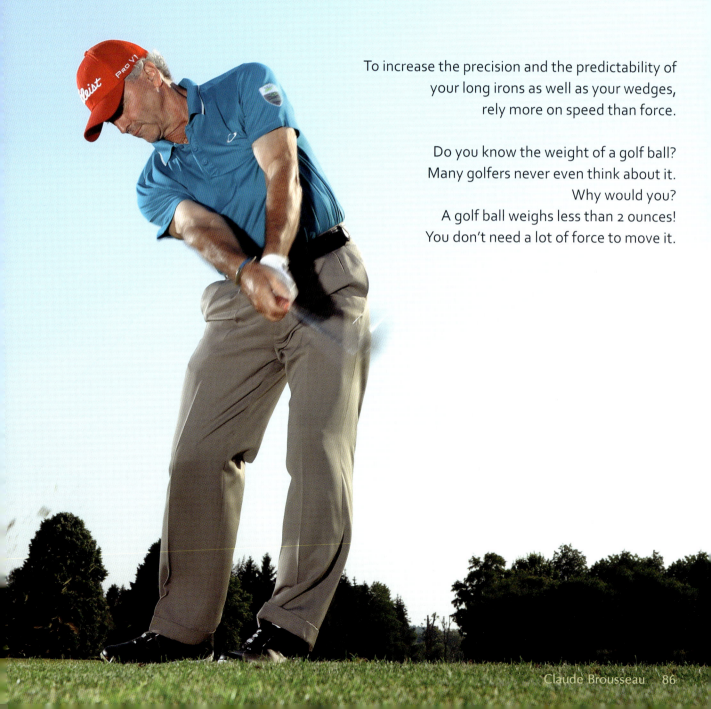

WEDGING

YOU NEED CLUB HEAD SPEED, NOT FORCE

To increase the precision and the predictability of
your long irons as well as your wedges,
rely more on speed than force.

Do you know the weight of a golf ball?
Many golfers never even think about it.
Why would you?
A golf ball weighs less than 2 ounces!
You don't need a lot of force to move it.

SPEED RATHER THAN FORCE

NO

Golfers are obsessed with distance. They want to hit the ball far. The further they want to hit it, the more force and muscular tension they use. It's as if they want to hit a bowling ball, yet a golf ball's weight is only 1.620 ounces. You will get much better results if you focus on speed rather than force. The real challenge in golf is controlling the distance and the trajectory of the ball. How good is it to hit the ball 185 yards when you only need to hit it 135? Next time you're on the course, just remember the ball is less than 2 ounces even when you swing your driver!

Focus on generating speed and solid contact. The result will be greater distance.

YES

2. THE GRIP

HOLD THE CLUB IN YOUR FINGERS

The first step for generating maximum velocity upon impact is a functional grip, how you hold the club.
The grip should rest more in your fingers and not so much in your palm.

A simple way to learn how to efficiently hold a golf club is to use a small ruler. To grasp the ruler, you will naturally have to use your fingers. Grasp the ruler several times and then do the same with the club. Over time, you will remember the PROficient grip.

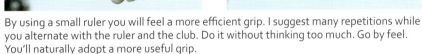

By using a small ruler you will feel a more efficient grip. I suggest many repetitions while you alternate with the ruler and the club. Do it without thinking too much. Go by feel. You'll naturally adopt a more useful grip.

Place the fingers first, then wrap the palm. The club is resting at the base of your index finger and below the heel pad of the palm. Close your hand on the grip.

MANAGE YOUR MUSCULAR TENSION

In golf, one of the worst enemies is excessive tension in the arms, shoulders and hands. To generate maximum speed, your muscles must be firm yet somewhat relaxed. Try this experiment:

1. Extend your trailing arm out in front of you and create as much tension as possible by vigorously clenching your fist. Attempt to move your arm swiftly.

2. Extend your arm out again and this time, relax it as much as you can, as if it's overcooked spaghetti! Once again, move your arm quickly.

Typically, in the first case, it will be very difficult to generate speed. In the second case, it should be a lot easier. Remember this image and these sensations when you swing. It should help you achieve an adequately relaxed muscular state to generate the maximum speed.

NO

If your arm is rigid, it's impossible to move it fast and create a lot of speed.

YES

If your arm is relaxed, you can move it swiftly and create speed.

STORAGE OF ENERGY AKA POWER!

Your goal is generating maximum speed at impact. You need to store energy during the backswing to be able to deliver it where it counts—when the club contacts the ball.

A good way to understand and feel what needs to happen is to picture yourself making a swing with one end of a rubber band on the grip and the other end under your leading foot. Loose at address, the rubber band (which represents the energy) will tighten progressively during the backswing to be fully extended at the top of the backswing (stored energy). You will feel powerful.

On the downswing, all the energy/power is released to "explode" upon impact. Therefore, on the backswing, you must accumulate energy by making a full shoulder rotation on a lower body that supports the load. By releasing that energy on the way down, you will get the most speed on impact without forcing it.

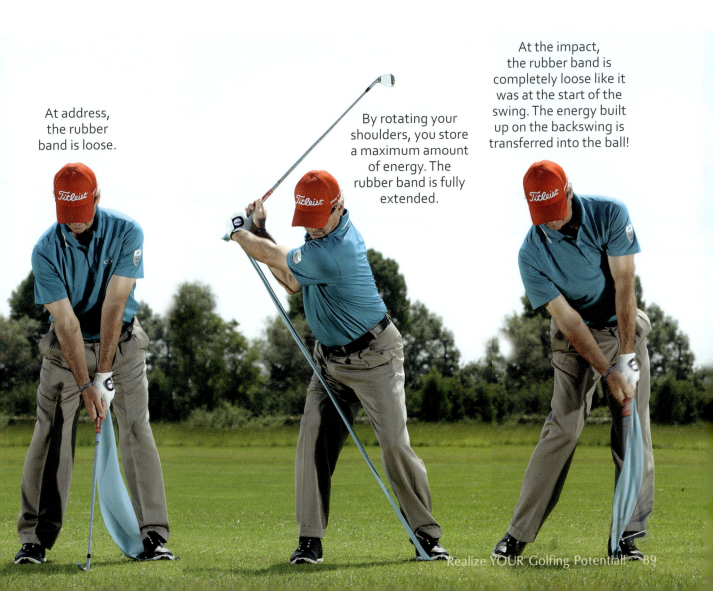

At address, the rubber band is loose.

By rotating your shoulders, you store a maximum amount of energy. The rubber band is fully extended.

At the impact, the rubber band is completely loose like it was at the start of the swing. The energy built up on the backswing is transferred into the ball!

MAINTAIN THE ANGLE

Another important source of speed is to hold the angle. During the downswing, the 90° angle formed between the leading arm and the club has to be held as long as possible before impact. Here is an exercise to make it happen: Make a backswing, then place 2 fingers of your trailing hand at the middle of the shaft, holding it with the tip of your fingers. Swing while holding back the shaft with your fingers. This will help maintain the angle between the lead arm and the club until right before impact. The more you hold the angle, the more you will generate speed upon impact without forcing it. You will experience effortless power!

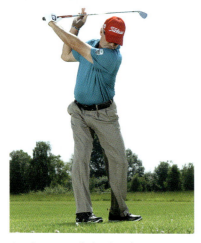

At the top of the backswing, place 2 fingers of your trailing hand on the middle of the shaft, holding it with the tip of your fingers.

Before impact, the angle between the lead arm and the club is maintained.

Release the club by turning your body to the left of the target.

6. THE IMPACT

AT FULL SPEED

We've seen that the maximum velocity of your swing must be reached at impact. The point of this exercise is to generate the loudest possible swish when the stick passes the point of impact. String together a dozen practice swings and then replicate the sensation when hitting a ball.

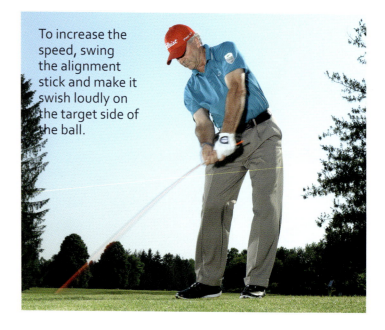

To increase the speed, swing the alignment stick and make it swish loudly on the target side of the ball.

LOB SHOTS

THE LOB SHOT IS THE LOVE SHOT!

We all love to see the ball flying high over an obstacle and land on the green like "a butterfly with sore feet."

This is a very useful shot to pop the ball over a shrub, a sand trap or a water hazard. The secondary benefit is that you will impress your playing partners with new skills.

TWO STEPS FOR A GOOD STANCE

With its high trajectory and quick stopping on the green, the lob is the ideal shot for getting over an obstacle. Yet many amateurs dread it for fear of chunking or topping the ball. Like every short game shot, THE SECRET TO SUCCESS depends on how well you get organized from the start. To set up properly every time, we recommend a 2-step process.

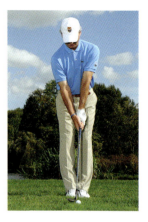

1. Stand with feet together. The ball is located slightly toward the lead foot. Use the sternum bone and the navel as a reference point. You will add loft on your wedge by opening the clubface.

2. Without moving the club, separate your feet slightly and open your stance. The alignment of your feet, hips and shoulders is about 30° to the left of the target line. Your weight distribution is 60% to 65% on the lead foot.

At address, the clubface is aimed at the intended target. It could be the flag or a landing zone depending on the green design and the hole location. Feet, hips and shoulders are oriented to the left. This creates an open stance. The grip and hands are always aligned with the middle of your body.

SWING IN LINE WITH YOUR BODY

Once you're well positioned, you need to swing along the same line as your shoulders and not along the target line as many players do. You also have to keep your clubface open from start to finish.

Important: Avoid introducing unnecessary movements upon impact. This way, you will reduce the risk of topping or chunking the ball. You need to trust the loft and use the bounce. These two elements are your best friends in this type of shot.

This shot requires a swing of significant length from the backswing to the finish in order to generate the necessary speed to lift the ball up high and stop it quickly on the green.

Swing in line with your body and finish with your hands high. The clubface remains at its original angle. You will complete the swing balanced on your lead leg as you watch the ball land on the green close to the hole.

USE A TENNIS RACQUET

For hitting good lob shots, a key element is maintaining, not only the clubface orientation established at address, but also the original loft during the entire swing. To best feel and understand this concept, I recommend making some practice swings with a tennis racquet. Mine has been lengthened, but this exercise works just as well with a regular racquet. The goal is to finish your swing with the racquet's grid facing the sky.

LOOK AT THE TOP OF THE FLAG

When hitting lob shots, a common mistake is to systematically land short of your target. The obstacle creates an optical illusion. The flag appears closer to you. To compensate for this, before hitting, imagine the ball dropping on top of the flagstick. To use an analogy with another sport, see a basketball dropping in the hoop.

1. Preset your brain and body by looking at the top of the flagstick.

2. Make a practice swing and hold the finish for a few seconds. Get a good feel for the speed of the club and keep looking at the top of the flagstick.

3. Play confidently with a positive attitude. In your mind, before the execution, the shot is always a success. You're good until proven otherwise. Commit 100% on the shot. Repeat this routine several times at the range, then use it as you need it on the course.

SAND, IT'S NOT THAT HARD

WHY IT'S THE EASIEST SHOT IN GOLF

Bunker shots are the easiest shots in golf? *Are you kidding me?* Actually, these shots are easier than you think as long as you have the right technique and understand how to use the bounce and the sand.

THE SET-UP IS 90% OF THE SHOT!

The ball should be slightly off the sternum bone toward the lead foot. The body should be perfectly parallel to the intended target line or slightly open. The bunker play, like all other golf shots, demands an irreproachable stance at address. When you practice, you must check your BPGA: BALL POSITION, POSTURE, GRIP and ALIGNMENT. Checking BPGA regularly when practicing helps avoid having to think about it when you're out on the course.

BALL The ball location is toward the target foot using the sternum as reference point. This allows the bottom of the swing to be in the sand behind the ball.

POSTURE 60% of the bodyweight is distributed to the lead foot. Feet are spread as wide as the hips or even the shoulders. Dig your feet into the sand, first for stability and second to have a feel for the texture of the sand.

GRIP Use a full-swing grip. The butt end of the grip points toward the center of the body. You don't necessarily have to slide your hands down on the grip.

ALIGNMENT The clubface orientation is not that important for the direction of the ball because the clubface doesn't come in contact with the ball. The more bounce you expose or use, the higher and shorter the ball will travel. The more you reduce the bounce, the more digging you will do and the ball will have a lower trajectory causing it to roll for a longer distance on the green. The feet, knees, hips and shoulders can be perfectly square or slightly open off the target line. A common mistake amateurs make is to open their stance and entire body too much.

THE BOUNCE IS YOUR BEST FRIEND!

You have to use it. The bounce is your insurance policy against a bad shot. To play a normal bunker shot, it's crucial to use the bounce of your wedge. The bounce makes the club "surf" on the sand. (I live in Hawaii!) The club will slide easily into the sand and propel the ball out of the bunker toward the target. However, if you don't have enough bounce, the leading edge of the club will dig into the sand too much and more often than not, the ball will stay in the sand.

The back of the club is lower than the leading edge. This is the bounce.

THROW SAND ON THE GREEN

Contrary to what many amateurs think, bunker shots aren't that difficult. In fact, it's the golf shot with the greatest margin of safety because the clubface never touches the ball! Before playing, your objective must be throwing sand on the green by letting the bounce of the sand wedge slide into the sand. At all cost, avoid scooping the ball with wrist action. The swing requires a decent club head speed. However, the average length of the greenside bunker shot is between 8 to 15 yards. You don't need to swing for 150 yards!

Most of the time, the amateur uses WAY TO MUCH energy for this type of shot. You can control the distance by simply adding more or less bounce without any other adjustment in the swing. Other ways of controlling the distance include: Use a different club, increase the length of the swing, increase the speed of the swing, take less or more sand.

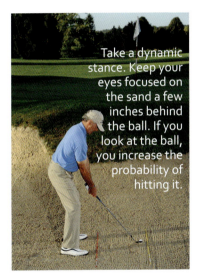

Take a dynamic stance. Keep your eyes focused on the sand a few inches behind the ball. If you look at the ball, you increase the probability of hitting it.

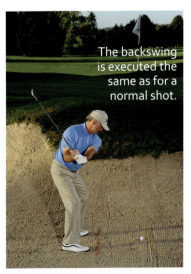

The backswing is executed the same as for a normal shot.

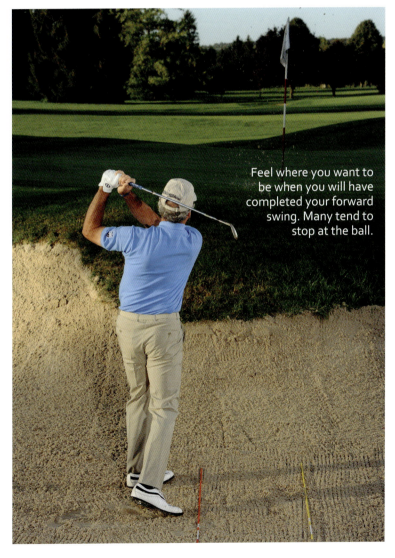

Feel where you want to be when you will have completed your forward swing. Many tend to stop at the ball.

A SMALL PILE OF SAND CAN DO YOU A LOT OF GOOD!

If you tend to top, chunk or scoop the ball when hitting a bunker shot, there's a simple training exercise that can help you improve quickly: Make a small pile of sand on the grass outside the bunker. Place the ball on top of the pile and take a classic greenside bunker stance described previously. Swing the club with the intention of propelling the sand forward. The explosion will automatically send the ball toward the intended target line.

This exercise is excellent for learning how to focus your mind on the sand.

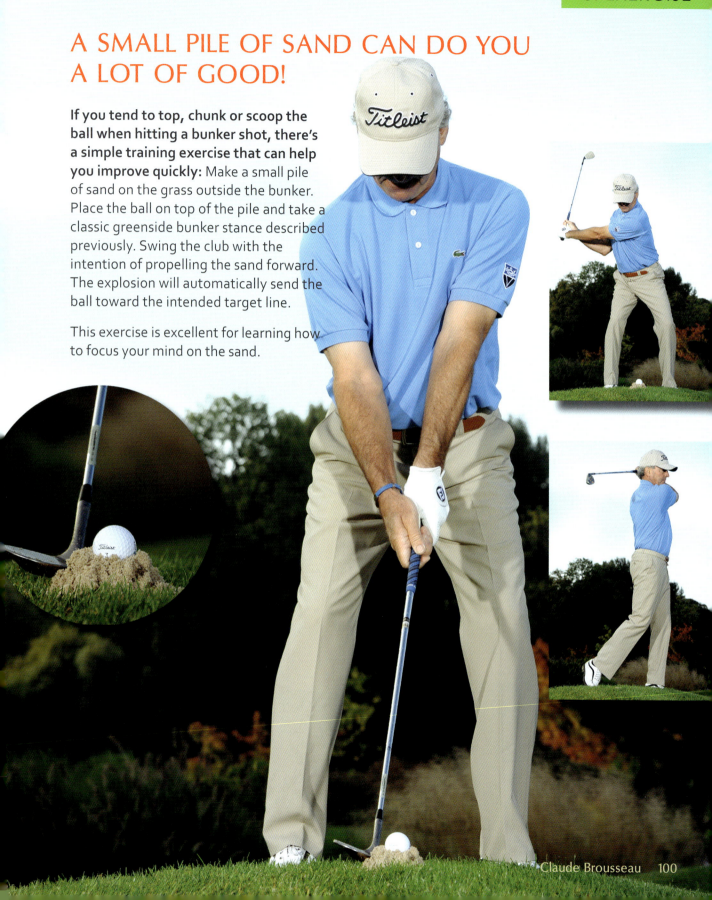

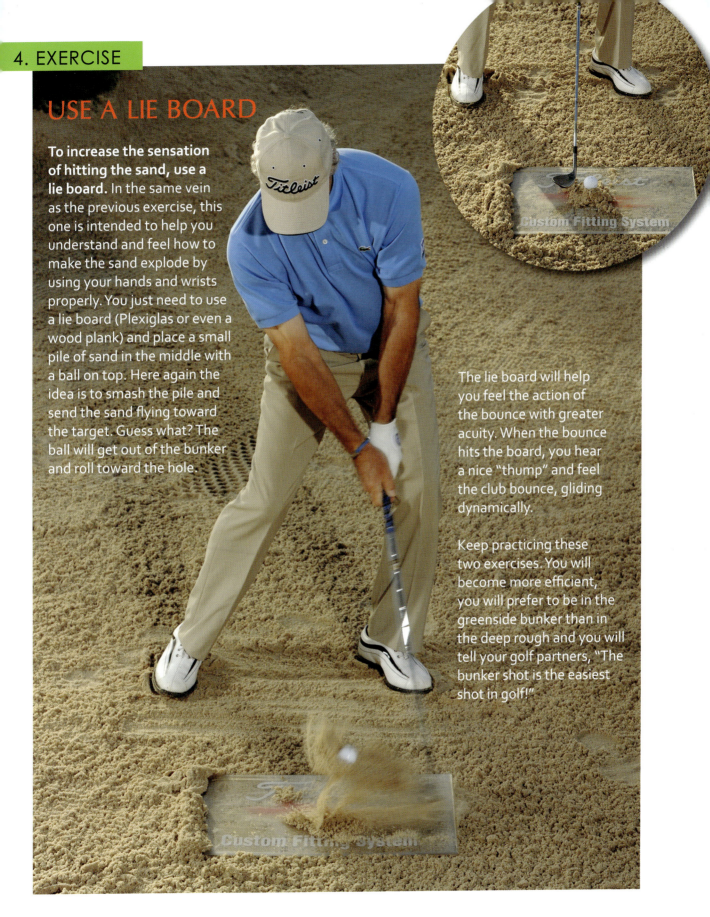

USE A LIE BOARD

To increase the sensation of hitting the sand, use a lie board. In the same vein as the previous exercise, this one is intended to help you understand and feel how to make the sand explode by using your hands and wrists properly. You just need to use a lie board (Plexiglas or even a wood plank) and place a small pile of sand in the middle with a ball on top. Here again the idea is to smash the pile and send the sand flying toward the target. Guess what? The ball will get out of the bunker and roll toward the hole.

The lie board will help you feel the action of the bounce with greater acuity. When the bounce hits the board, you hear a nice "thump" and feel the club bounce, gliding dynamically.

Keep practicing these two exercises. You will become more efficient, you will prefer to be in the greenside bunker than in the deep rough and you will tell your golf partners, "The bunker shot is the easiest shot in golf!"

GREENSIDE BUNKER

MEET YOUR TWO
NEW BEST FRIENDS:
THE BOUNCE AND THE SAND

Amateurs are very apprehensive of the greenside bunker.
Most of them have a misconception of how to use
the bounce (Friend Number 1) and the sand (Friend Number 2).

BOUNCE OR LEADING EDGE?

It depends on the lie and the texture of the sand. The bunker shot is the golf shot that provides players with the greatest margin of error. The clubface never touches the ball, and the contact in the sand can be in different places and the ball will still fly out. As a result, no matter what direction the clubface is oriented, the ball will fly in a straight line parallel to your body orientation.

The basic principle can be broken down into three parts: The club hits the sand, it generates an explosion and the explosion propels the ball onto the green.

The other important point for making a successful bunker shot is to properly use your sand wedge's bounce or leading edge. The decision is based on two factors: The lie of the ball (good lie or plugged) and the texture of the sand (fluffy or hardpan).

ORIGINAL BOUNCE ANGLE

INCREASED BOUNCE ANGLE

INCREASE THE BOUNCE

If your ball has a good lie and especially if the sand is very fluffy, you need to increase the bounce angle of your sand wedge at address. I suggest you lower your hands at the address. This action will allow the club to slide in the sand. The higher the bounce angle, the shorter the distance the ball will fly and the higher the ball trajectory will be.

Now it's time to get ready! Let's explore how you will set up. There are many ways to achieve the same result. I am proposing a few simple steps that YOU, the CEO of YOUR golf swing, can adapt according to your preferences. It's always about performance!

- Place your clubface behind the ball with its original bounce angle without touching the sand.
- Without moving your leading hand, release the grip pressure and increase the bounce angle by spinning the grip clockwise with your trailing hand. Then reposition your trailing hand to obtain a secure, steady, firm grip.
- It's important that the butt end of the club remains oriented in the center of your body.
- Lower your hands a few inches below your normal address position.
- You should have a fairly good amount of knee flex by squatting to shallow the angle of attack.

ORIGINAL BOUNCE ANGLE

Place the clubface behind the ball (without touching the sand!) while maintaining the original angle.

INCREASED BOUNCE ANGLE

After having increased the bounce angle by spinning the grip clockwise, make sure your hands are in the middle of your body or just slightly toward the target groin.

ORIGINAL BOUNCE ANGLE

INCREASED BOUNCE ANGLE

THE SWING

With a good lie, it is easier to produce a good shot!
Once you're in a good position, look a few inches in the sand behind the ball. This will be the point of entrance in the sand.

Commit and execute a rhythmic swing to a balanced finishing position. The backswing and the follow through are executed on a typical swing plane. The divot is shallow, and the ball flies on the green toward your target.

At the finish, the player is balanced and the body has rotated properly. The divot is shallow. Remember, it is a finesse shot. The average distance of a greenside bunker is less than 15 yards.

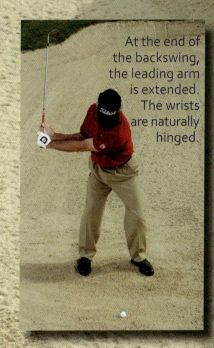

At the end of the backswing, the leading arm is extended. The wrists are naturally hinged.

The club hits the sand a few inches behind the ball.

WITH A PLUGGED BALL. . .

If your ball is plugged, you have to reduce your sand wedge's bounce angle at address. This action will lead to a deeper divot into the sand because you are using the leading edge of the sand wedge. The ball is lower in the sand, you need to dig it out. You will move a greater amount of sand. The ball trajectory will be lower and the ball will roll a greater distance on the green. You will need to adjust your landing zone accordingly.

ORIGINAL BOUNCE ANGLE

DECREASE THE BOUNCE ANGLE

. . .IT'S TIME FOR SOME DIGGING!

Now it's time to get ready! Let's explore how you will set up. There are many ways to achieve the same result. I'm proposing a few simple steps that YOU, the CEO of YOUR golf swing, can adapt according to your preferences. It's always about performance!

- ⚑ Without touching the sand, place your clubface behind the ball using the original bounce angle.
- ⚑ Without moving your leading hand, release the grip pressure and decrease the bounce angle by spinning the grip counterclockwise with your trailing hand. Then reposition your trailing hand to obtain a firm, steady grip.
- ⚑ It's important that the butt end of the club remains oriented in the center of your body.
- ⚑ Keep your hands in a normal address position.

Keep the grip the same. Use the leading edge to dig the ball out.

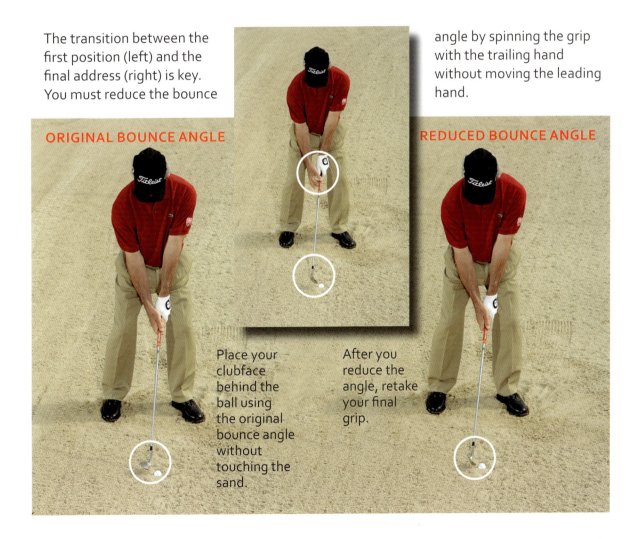

The transition between the first position (left) and the final address (right) is key. You must reduce the bounce angle by spinning the grip with the trailing hand without moving the leading hand.

ORIGINAL BOUNCE ANGLE

REDUCED BOUNCE ANGLE

Place your clubface behind the ball using the original bounce angle without touching the sand.

After you reduce the angle, retake your final grip.

THE SWING

With a plugged ball, you can execute the backswing the same way you do with a normal shot. You can use a slightly steeper swing plane if you prefer. Since the club is digging into the sand, the divot will be deeper. You will move a greater amount of sand. The finish will be slightly shortened because of the high resistance of the sand.

The success of a greenside bunker shot is predetermined by the quality of the set up and understanding how to use the bounce appropriately.

The follow through is shorter because of the digging action. The divot is deep.

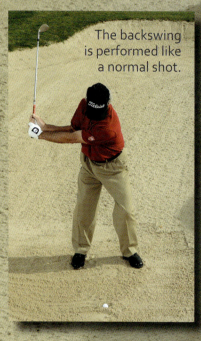

The backswing is performed like a normal shot.

The club hits the sand a few inches before the ball.

LONG BUNKER SHOTS

KNOW YOUR OPTIONS
TO MEET THE CHALLENGE

You have missed the green and your ball is in a bunker 20 to 30 yards from the green. These shots are often qualified as the most difficult shots in golf. Not anymore!

Here is the goal: Successfully hitting a low trajectory ball which rolls and finishes near the flag. Then you make the putt and save your par.

BALL IN THE MIDDLE, SQUARE STANCE

For long bunker shots between 20 and 30 yards, I recommend using a gap wedge, pitching wedge and sometimes you can even swing a 9 iron. The idea is that with slightly less loft the ball will have a lower trajectory and will roll more on the green. You must take into consideration the height of the lip. You want to make sure you have enough lift to carry over it.

You will need a few adjustments in the set up. At address, you should place the ball toward the middle of your body. Keep your hands in the middle of your body. Keep the clubface perpendicular to the intended target line. Keep your body parallel to the target line. You can have your leading foot open 20°. This will facilitate the hips' rotation in the follow through swing. I recommend a weight distribution on your feet of 50%/50%. You will dig your feet slightly into the sand to feel the texture and stabilize the lower body. Focus on the sand a few inches behind the ball. You're ready to swing!

A "FLAT" AND "LOW" SWING

On a long bunker shot, it's more efficient to use a shallower backswing. It will feel like a more rounded swing. As far as the follow through, you will be more PROficient with a low follow through. You MUST resist the temptation to lift the ball. Most of the time, the action of lifting the ball will result in disastrous "fat" shots.

For a normal bunker shot, you need to look at the sand a few inches behind the ball.

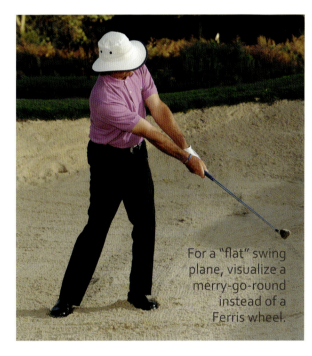

For a "flat" swing plane, visualize a merry-go-round instead of a Ferris wheel.

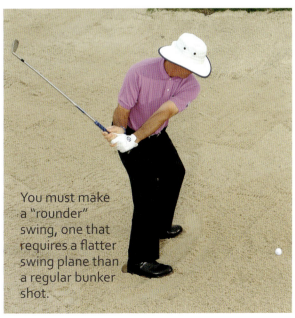

You must make a "rounder" swing, one that requires a flatter swing plane than a regular bunker shot.

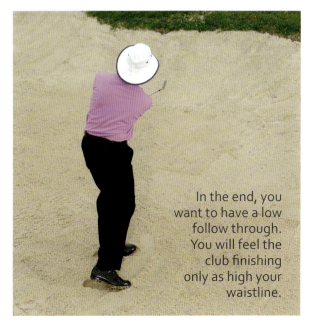

In the end, you want to have a low follow through. You will feel the club finishing only as high your waistline.

CHECK YOUR SWING PLANE

We've seen that a long bunker shot requires a fairly flat swing plane. Now you need feedback to make sure this is what you're doing. An easy way to make sure the plane is more efficient is by using an alignment stick. Place the alignment stick over your grip. Hold it firmly with your hands. This will create an extension of the shaft. Set up at address ready to swing. Make a slow backswing while checking your swing plane. If it's PROficient, or flat enough, the end of the stick will point beyond the ball. If the plane is too vertical, the end of the stick will point somewhere between your feet and the ball.

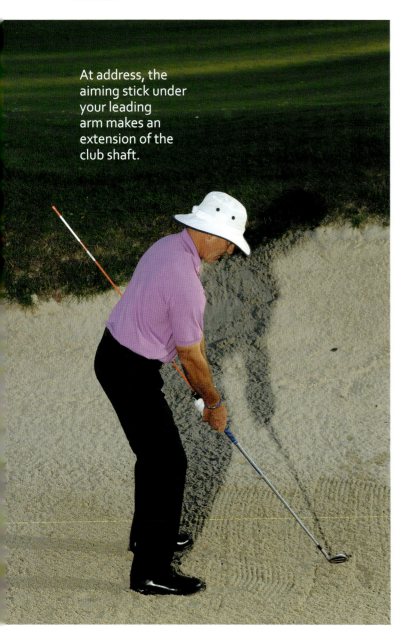

At address, the aiming stick under your leading arm makes an extension of the club shaft.

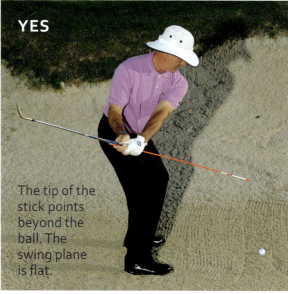

YES

The tip of the stick points beyond the ball. The swing plane is flat.

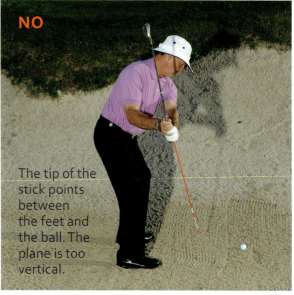

NO

The tip of the stick points between the feet and the ball. The plane is too vertical.

CONTROL THE LENGTH OF YOUR BACKSWING

To successfully execute a long bunker shot, the other important technical aspect is to control the amplitude and the length of your backswing. You will need to practice to imprint the feel. An effective way of memorizing the right position is to practice by doing three things:

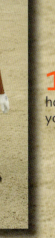

1. Stand at address holding the club with your trailing arm.

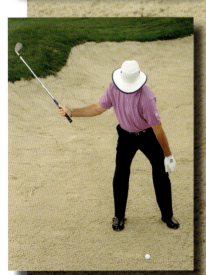

2. Make your backswing with the trailing hand only on the club while feeling "long" and "flat."

3. Reach for the grip with the leading hand. Take your time and feel the length of the swing. You can close your eyes to increase your awareness. Use this acquired sensation when you are on the course. It's critical to remember the primary objective is to splash the sand. Its displacement propels the ball toward the landing area or the flag.

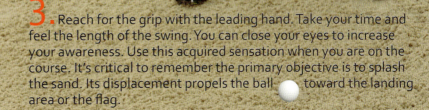

MASTER YOUR PROCESS

INFORMATION, DECISION, ACTION, EVALUATION

Be the best at YOUR process!

In golf, technique isn't everything. Your shot preparation, commonly known as your "Pre-shot Routine," is just as important for becoming a highly skilled player. There are two distinct areas that require distinctive skills. Using the terminology of VISION54, we'll call them the **Think Box** and the **Play Box.**

THE ANALYSIS

When you stand in front of the ball, the first thing to do is analyze the overall situation. This phase has five steps: assessing the lie, measuring the distance, adjusting the distance, choosing the trajectory and selecting a club. This all happens while standing a few yards behind the ball, a place we'll call the Think Box. It can be done in a matter of seconds. Nobody likes slow players! This will satisfy your need for thinking.

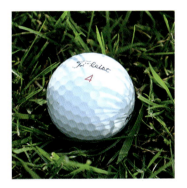

1. ASSESSING THE LIE

The first step of the analysis is to examine the lie of the ball. Where is the ball resting? Is it perfectly positioned in the fairway or is it in a divot? Is it in light or heavy rough? Is it in uphill, downhill or side hill? Is it on a flat area in the bunker or sitting inside a footprint? The answer to these questions will let you determine what type of shot you can make and which club to use. It's a crucial step toward making a great shot. You have to adjust your expectation of the result according to the quality of the lie.

2. MEASURING THE DISTANCE

The second action is to measure the distance. There are many devices and tools to assist you such as fairway markers, yardage books, GPS devices and range finders. Whichever you use, be mindful of the difference between the distance to the front edge of the green and the distance to the flag. It can sometimes be more than 30 yards! Even though professionals insist on knowing the front and back of the green plus to the flag, I recommend you concern yourself only with the back of the green if you have a handicap/index higher than 15. Why? Because recreational golfers rarely take enough club for the distance they need the ball to travel. We'll call it the "starting" distance.

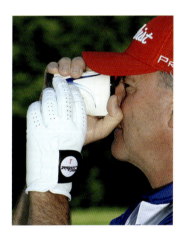

3. ADJUSTING THE DISTANCE

For a given distance and player, the club selection can range from a 9 iron to a 3 wood! It depends on the terrain and the weather conditions. Two elements are crucial: the wind speed/direction and the difference in elevation between your ball and the green. If you're hitting downwind, you may have to subtract 10 to 30 yards from your "starting" distance. If hitting into the wind, you may have to add 10 to 30 yards. A good rule of thumb is 10 yards for every 10 miles per hour wind speed. Similarly, if the green is above your ball, you might add 10 to 30 yards, and if it's below your ball, you will subtract 10 to 30 yards. Again here you can use the 10/10 rules: 10 yards for 10 feet of elevation. This is a very good starting point. You also have to adjust for the rain, the cold and the altitude. Once all these elements have been factored in, do the calculation relative to your "starting" distance to determine a new "adjusted" distance to the flag.

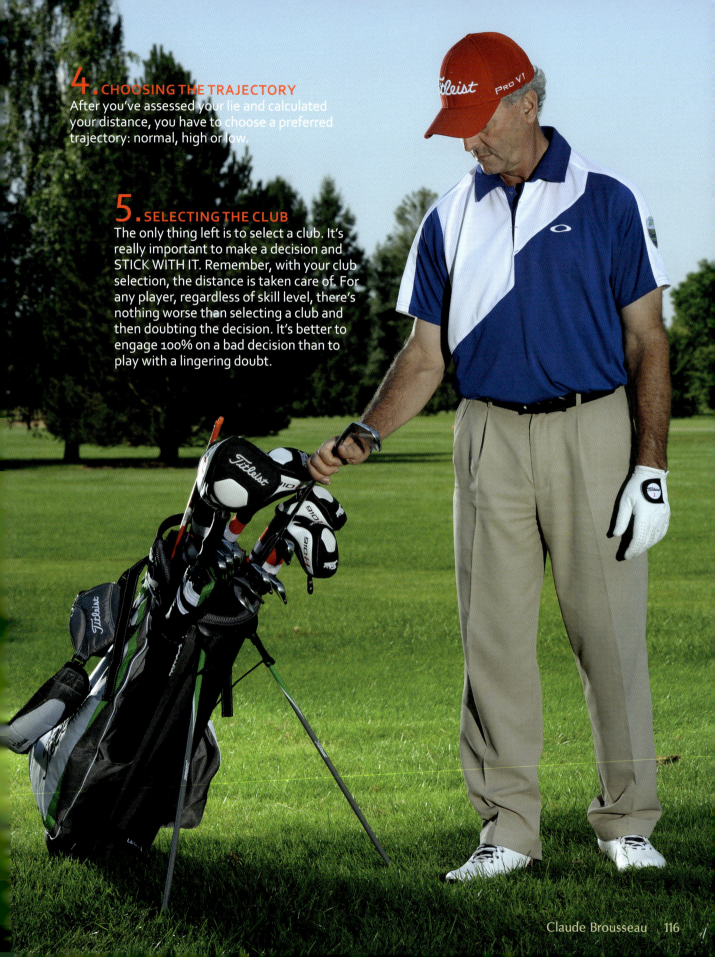

4. CHOOSING THE TRAJECTORY

After you've assessed your lie and calculated your distance, you have to choose a preferred trajectory: normal, high or low.

5. SELECTING THE CLUB

The only thing left is to select a club. It's really important to make a decision and STICK WITH IT. Remember, with your club selection, the distance is taken care of. For any player, regardless of skill level, there's nothing worse than selecting a club and then doubting the decision. It's better to engage 100% on a bad decision than to play with a lingering doubt.

FINAL STEPS

Once you've selected a club, stay in the Think Box a few yards behind or on the side of the ball. There you will make a practice swing. Remember the feel of the best swing you've performed with this club in a similar situation.

1. THE PRACTICE SWING

The purpose of a practice swing is to get ready to play. For some, it can just be a way to loosen up the muscles; for others, it's a true re-creation of the actual swing. For the short game, 2 or 3 practice swings can be required to get a feel for the right length and speed of the swing or even for just finding the bottom of the swing. You don't need to do a practice swing if your gut feeling is sending you signals that you are ready.

2. VISUALIZATION

The last action taken in the Think Box could be the visualization of the shot, either by imagining the trajectory, picturing the ball reaching the green or seeing yourself play through the entire shot. Some golfers can't visualize, so don't worry about it. As long as you have a sense of feeling how you want to move your body and the club, you will be fine. You will make a decision on what you want to feel in the Play Box. It could be hearing the club contacting the ball, it could be balance, it could be the tempo of the swing. You need to explore what sense produces the best performance.

3. ALIGNMENT AND AIMING

Locate a point not more than 3 feet in front of the ball, which serves as a guide for lining up the clubface relative to the target. You can locate a second point parallel to the first one to serve as a reference for aligning your body.

THE ACTION

In the Play Box, it's "Show Time." Spend only the time required for the task at hand: swinging the club and making solid contact. Spend as little time as possible in the Play Box. That way, there's less time for distracting thoughts and less time for unnecessary muscular tension to build up. In the Play Box, you're more in a "sensory" mode than an "intellectual" mode. You're an athlete swinging a club to move an object that's less than 2 ounces from Point A to Point B.

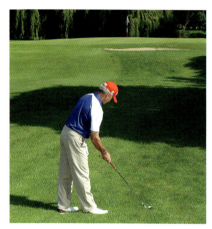

1. SET UP

You're now in the Play Box. You aim the club head in relation to an imaginary target you've chosen. You focus only on this one action.

2. FINAL ADDRESS

Once the club head is lined up, you align your body parallel to the target line. You look at your target one last time. You're fully engaged and focused on that target.

3. EXECUTION

Your eyes return to the ball and you immediately swing the club to play your shot with full confidence. You assess the result. If you're happy with it, bank it in your memory bank of good shots! This is how you build confidence. Next time, you can access it. You will produce good shots on-demand. You will walk toward your ball and repeat the same sequence of "decision and action" for the next shot. In between shots, send your brain on vacation.

*The Think Box® Decision Line® and Play Box® by Pia Nilsson and Lynn Marriott of Vision54. Used with permission.

CONCLUSION

You now have the "intellectual knowledge" for producing good shots on-demand, and the photographs to provide great visual support for experiencing the "sensory knowledge."

It's time to take action!
Use this information at the practice facility and even more importantly, on the course.
You want to minimize the variables so always remember that simple is better.
It doesn't mean easy.

Stay focused on what is under your control.
Learn to manage the variability of golf.
And keep having fun while **YOU REALIZE YOUR GOLFING POTENTIAL**!

Warmest Aloha!

Claude Brousseau

ABOUT THE AUTHOR

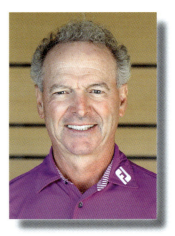

I grew up in a small town located 425 miles northwest of Montréal, Québec, Canada. Not only are the winters very long, summers last only 24 hours. Just kidding! Hockey is the national sport so the dream of every kid is to become an NHL player. I never played golf as a kid.

Golf is my third life. I graduated with a Bachelors Degree in Nursing and worked primarily in intensive care units. After several years in the medical field, I decided to go back to school, graduating with an MBA. I worked in real estate investment and management, buying and managing shopping centers and office buildings for investors.

I started to play golf as a hobby. Before I knew it I was hooked! I love the game and the challenge it represents. The real deal came when I traveled to Glen Abbey and witnessed my first PGA Tour tournament: the Canadian Open. I vividly remember Jack Nicklaus hitting at least 20 drives without having to re-adjust the tee. Payne Stewart, Tom Watson, Lee Trevino and many of the big names were all there. I wanted to become a PGA player. It was a foolish dream for a 30 year-old guy who had never even come close to shooting par.

In November 1992 I moved to Fort Lauderdale, Florida with the intent of becoming a scratch golfer and compete with the best. I searched for the top teachers, took numerous lessons and worked extremely hard on my game. I became a golf addict. I read countless books, listened to audiotapes and watched videos. I had a coach for my short game, long game and mental game. I had to find a way to make it happen. I worked 16-hour days at the hospital Saturdays and Sundays so I could golf the rest of the week.

My first round under par came in 1995 at Lago Mar Country Club in Fort Lauderdale, Florida after years of dedicated practice. My best round was 68 on the Players Course at Weston Hill Country Club, Weston, Florida. I played professionally with very limited success on the South Florida Golf Tour and the Montgomery Coca Cola Golf Tour. I played in the Monday qualifiers for the Doral Open and the Honda Classic. It didn't take long for me to realize my true passion was teaching, not competing.

In 1998 I began teaching full time. Since then I've taught in Florida, North Carolina, Canada, France, Belgium, Luxembourg and Hawaii where I currently live and instruct. I had the privilege of coaching players on the European Tour, Challenge Tour, Alps Tour, European Senior Tour, Ladies European Tour and with several collegiate players. I also enjoyed the role of assistant coach to the Lahainaluna High School girl's team for a few years. I love introducing juniors to the best game in the world.

In 2009, thanks to Jean-Claude Forestier, the opportunity of a lifetime came my way. I was given the privilege of creating the first short game golf school in France from the ground up. It was the perfect occasion to showcase the expertise I acquired while teaching at over ten different golf schools

in the U.S. We help thousands of golfers revolutionize their short game. The Golf Court Academy is renowned as the place to enhance your scoring skills.

I obtained my PGA Class A in June 2003, my Certification in Teaching & Coaching in January 2011 and finally my Masters in June 2014. My peers voted me Aloha Section PGA Teacher of the Year twice in 2008 and 2015. I was awarded the 2014 Aloha Section PGA Bill Strausbaugh Award and in 2016 Aloha Section Horton Smith Award. *Golf Digest* honored me with the 2015-2016 Best Teachers in your state. I was ranked #3 in the state of Hawaii.

In 2015, I became a member of the Golf Channel Academy. I was selected among the game's most influential and recognized teachers, who that year came together to establish a dedicated network of instruction facilities with the active support of Golf Channel, the game's leading global multimedia and golf entertainment source.

I was featured on *Golf Channel Morning Drive*, KFVE K5 TV, TVA in Canada, Canal+ TV in France and I've been a regular guest on Danielle Tucker's *The Golf Club Radio Show* in Hawaii, as well as ESPN *Radio Honolulu*. More than 60 of my articles have been published in several golf magazines in the U.S., Europe and Canada, and I've produced two DVDs and more than 15 videos with Golf Channel.

I'm passionate about helping golfers "Realize YOUR Golfing Potential." I feel blessed every day to be able to interact with golfers from all over the world. I'm very grateful that they trust my expertise.

Living on Maui has been a dream of mine since the first time I visited the island in 1988. It took patience and perseverance, like golf, to finally move to paradise in November 2005 where I currently instruct at Maui School of Golf/Golf Channel Academy located at Kahili Golf Course. The "Aloha Spirit" suits my soul.

I have been fortunate and I am eternally grateful to my wife, Anne-Marie, who has always been my number one fan and has supported me 100% on this crazy adventure!

Enjoy this book, keep learning and most importantly, have fun on the course!

Warmest Aloha,

www.mauischoolofgolf.com

Claude Brousseau
PGA Master

PRODUCT RESOURCES

For more information on any of the fine products mentioned in this book, please visit their websites:

AIMPOINT®
WWW.AIMPOINTGOLF.COM

CHIPINABLE®
WWW.CHIPINABLE.COM

IDL STROKE PUTTING TRACK®
WWW.MOMENTUSSPORTS.COM

STIMPMETER®
WWW.USGA.ORG

SWEET SPOT 360®
WWW. EYELINEGOLF.COM

TALY®
WWW.TALY.COM

THE THINK BOX® DECISION LINE® PLAY BOX®
WWW. VISION54.COM

WHIPPY PUTTER®
WWW.TEMPOMASTER.COM